BX
1751.2
.R3413
1997

SALT OF THE EARTH

Joseph Cardinal Ratzinger

Salt of the Earth

Christianity and the Catholic Church
at the End of the Millennium

An Interview with Peter Seewald

Translated by Adrian Walker

CCU Library
8787 W. Alameda Ave.
Lakewood, CO 80226

IGNATIUS PRESS   SAN FRANCISCO

Title of the German original:
*Salz der Erde: Christentum und katholische Kirche
an der Jahrtausendwende*
© 1996 Deutsche Verlags-Anstalt GmbH, Stuttgart

Cover photograph by Hermann Dornhege,
I.G. Bildarchiv

Cover design by Roxanne Mei Lum

© 1997 Ignatius Press, San Francisco
All rights reserved
ISBN 0–89870–640–8
Library of Congress catalogue number 97–70806
Printed in the United States of America ∞

Contents

PART 3

On the Threshold of a New Era

Foreword

Rome in winter. The people in Saint Peter's Square were wearing coats and clasping their umbrellas. In the cafés people were drinking tea, and as I visited a grave in the Campo Santo even the cats were wailing [about the cold].

As usual, on Saturday the Cardinal was still at work in his office. We planned to drive afterward to the region of Frascati, to a former Jesuit residence called the Villa Cavalletti. The chauffeur was waiting at the curb in a Mercedes that the Congregation for the Doctrine of the Faith had bought secondhand a few years earlier in Germany. I was standing there with a huge suitcase, as if I were about to take a trip around the world. The door finally opened, and a modest, very white-haired, and slightly fragile-looking man came out with short steps. He wore a black suit with a clerical collar and carried a minuscule, simple suitcase.

I had left the Church a long time before; there were plenty of reasons. Once upon a time, all you had to do was sit in a church, and you got bombarded by particles of faith loaded in the course of centuries. But now every certainty had become questionable, and all tradition seemed impossibly old and stale. Some were of the opinion that religion had to adapt to people's needs. Others thought that Christianity had outlived its usefulness; it was out of date and no longer had a right to exist. It is not altogether easy to leave the Church.

But it is even less easy to return. Does God really exist? And if so, do we need a Church as well? What is it supposed to look like—and how can someone rediscover it?

The Cardinal never asked me about my past or my current status. He didn't want to look at any of the questions beforehand, nor did he request that anything be omitted or added. The atmosphere of our meeting was intense and serious, but sometimes this "prince of the Church" sat so casually on his chair, one foot on the crossbar, that you might have thought you were talking with a student. Once he interrupted the conversation to retire for a meditation, or maybe to ask the Holy Spirit for the right words. I don't know.

Joseph Cardinal Ratzinger is considered, especially in his homeland, a combative but also controversial churchman. However, many of his early analyses and assessments have proved true, often in detail. And few people are more painfully aware of the losses and the drama of the Church than this shrewd man of simple background from rural Bavaria.

At one point I asked him how many ways to God there were. I really didn't know what he would answer. He could have said, "only one" or "several". The Cardinal didn't take long to answer: As many, he said, as there are people.

PETER SEEWALD

Munich, August 15, 1996

The Catholic Faith: Words and Signs

Your Eminence, it is said that the Pope is afraid of you. He asks himself: For heaven's sake, what would Cardinal Ratzinger say about that?

(Ratzinger, amused): He might say that jokingly, but he is definitely not afraid of me!

Is there a certain ceremonial when you meet with the Pope?

No.

Do you pray first?

No, I'm afraid I must confess that we don't; we sit down together at the table.

So you come in and shake hands?

Yes. First I wait; then the Pope comes in. We shake hands, sit down together at the table, and have a little personal chat that doesn't have anything to do with theology per se. Normally I then present what I want to say, the Pope asks whatever questions he has, and this starts another conversation going.

Does he make very concrete remarks?

It depends on the topic. There are some subjects where he basically waits to see what we have to say. An example is the question about how to admit converted Anglicans into the Catholic Church. It's necessary to find juridical forms for that. In this case, he intervenes very little but says only, "Be generous." But the details of the procedure don't interest him so much. Then there are other topics in which he has a very lively interest, such as everything having to do with morality, whether bioethics or social ethics, the whole sphere of philosophy, everything that somehow touches on philosophy. Or the whole sphere of catechesis and doctrine. That interests him very personally, and there are really intense discussions on those points.

What do you wear when you meet?

The cassock. It's the tradition to meet the Pope in a cassock.

And the Pope?

He wears a white cassock.

In what language do you converse?

We speak German.

Not Latin?

No.

A pious visitor from the Protestant community of the Hutterites once

addressed you with the words "Brother Joseph". Did you find that
inappropriate, if not disrespectful? After all, in customary Catholic
usage you are addressed as "Your Eminence".

No, I think "Brother Joseph" is quite all right. It's not our
style of speaking, but if we talk about the brotherhood of
Christians—in 1960 I wrote a short book about Christian
brotherhood—then it's very much in line with something I
have tried to keep in mind from very early on in my life.

Does a cardinal have certain higher demands to live up to, higher, I
mean, than those placed on, say, a priest or an archbishop?

A cardinal is a Christian, a priest, and a bishop. He is someone
who has a responsibility in the Church to see that the gospel is
being proclaimed and the sacraments are being celebrated. I
wouldn't simply accept the phrase "higher demands". I would
say instead that there are very specific demands on a cardinal.
Even a parish priest, a simple country priest, has very heavy
demands made of him, in that he has to understand people
and assist them in sickness, grief, and joy, at marriages and
funerals, in crises and in moments of joy. He has to try to believe with them and to keep the ship of the Church on course.

Isn't it extremely wearing having to deal with God every day?
Doesn't one get sick and tired of it?

Dealing with God every day is a necessity for me. For just as
we have to breathe every day, just as we need light every day
and have to eat every day, just as we also need friendship every
day and truly need certain people every day, dealing with God
is one of the absolutely fundamental elements of life. If God
suddenly disappeared, my soul wouldn't be able to breathe

properly. In that sense there is no boredom here. It can occur when it comes to certain pious practices, in relation to certain devotional readings, but not in relation to God as such.

Still, it's no doubt also true that one doesn't automatically become more just and gentle or wiser and more faithful by occupying oneself with God and the Church.

Unfortunately, that's true. By itself studying theology doesn't make a person better. It helps to make him better when he doesn't pursue it just as a theory but tries to get a better understanding of himself and of man and the world as a whole in what he reads and then tries to appropriate it as a form of life. But in itself theology is primarily an intellectual occupation, above all when it is pursued with scholarly rigor and seriousness. It can have repercussions on one's attitude as a human being, but it doesn't necessarily make man better as such.

Are there demands of Jesus that are hard even for a cardinal to fulfill?

Most certainly, because he is just as weak as other people, and his position, with its varied responsibilities, may even get him into more serious trouble. I would say that all ten commandments, which are summed up in the great commandment of love, are ones that he, like anyone else, never completely fulfills. It is, in fact, often hard to love, to love God and man, and to do it in a way that is in keeping with the Word of God. There is no doubt about that at all, and we know well enough from history how weak cardinals can be in this respect.

So it's sometimes hard even for a cardinal to love people.

You know, you can't love people collectively anyway. Of course, there are unlikable types whom it is very difficult to love. And sometimes one can almost begin to doubt whether the person is good and to ask oneself whether the Creator hasn't let things get so far out of hand that this creature is starting to become dangerous and can't be worthy of love any longer. But then one has to say: Some I don't know at all, so I am not competent to make a judgment about them, and the others I have to leave as they are. And the good people I know constantly reassure me that the Creator does in fact know what he has done.

Do you go to confession? Do you have your own confessor?

Yes. That, I think, is necessary for all of us.

Does this mean that even a cardinal does things that are wrong?

It's there for all to see.

Do you sometimes feel helpless and overtaxed or lonely, like other people do?

Yes. Precisely in my present position, my strength is far from equal to what I am really supposed to do. And the older one gets, the more one suffers from the fact that one simply doesn't have sufficient strength to do what one is supposed to do; that one is too weak and helpless, or not up to situations. And then one says to God, now you must help, I can't go on. There is loneliness as well. However, I would say that the Lord has—thank goodness—put so many fine people in my path that I never have to feel completely alone.

Since 1981 you have been Prefect of the Congregation for the Doc-trine of the Faith. Not only is the CDF the oldest congregation in the Vatican, but as the "Holy Inquisition" it was for centuries the most feared as well. Your job is to maintain the purity of the Catholic faith, to defend the Church against heresies, and even to punish offenses against the faith if the need arises. Does this mean that everything the Prefect of the CDF says is automatically the teaching of the Church?

Of course not. I would never presume to use the decisions of the Congregation to impose my own theological ideas on the Christian people. I really try to exercise restraint in this area, and I see my role as that of a coordinator of a large working group.

You might say, in fact, that we work in large concentric circles. There is a worldwide correspondence with theologians who advise us. We have contacts with the bishops and their agencies. In addition, we have our theologians in Rome, the Theological Commission, the Biblical Commission. Then there is the advisory body proper, the so-called *Consulta*, and, finally, the cardinals, who make the decisions. And it is only in these large concentric circles that decisions can ripen.

When the cardinals meet, we never make decisions if the consultors aren't in substantial agreement, because we say that if there are markedly different opinions among good theologians, then we can't declare by some higher light, as it were, that only one is right. Only when the advisory team has come to at least a large degree of unanimity, a basic convergence, do we make decisions as well.

But there are also things that you can present definitely as your private opinion.

Of course. After all, I worked for many years as a professor, and I still try as best I can to keep up with the theological discussion. Naturally, I have my own ideas about how theology should look; I also express them in my own publications.

Might it not also be the case that Cardinal Ratzinger would have to contradict himself on occasion? I mean that, on the one hand, you express a private opinion about an issue that as Prefect you might not be able to hold?

Let's put it this way: time can certainly bring correction. I can simply learn through dialogue that I haven't seen this or that matter properly. On the other hand, I couldn't deny a present conviction that I had reached to the best of my abilities. That isn't possible, you see. On the other hand, a development through further learning that also brings a correction of past views is entirely within the realm of possibility.

As it stands, many of your warnings and appeals have plainly borne all too little fruit. At any rate, you haven't managed to bring about a broad movement against the currents of our time and a general change of mentality. You have found consolation in the thought that God leads the Church by mysterious paths. But isn't it depressing that the discussion keeps going around in circles, that the level of the debate has actually sunk further? In the meantime it even seems that the substance of the faith has increasingly gone to ruin, that there is now even greater indifference with respect to all issues.

I never imagined that I could, so to speak, redirect the rudder of history. And if our Lord himself ends up on the Cross, one sees that God's ways do not lead immediately to measurable successes. This, I think, is really very important. The disciples asked him certain questions: What's going on, why aren't we getting anywhere? And he answered with the parables about the mustard seed, the leaven, and the like, telling them that statistics is not one of God's measurements. In spite of that, something essential and crucial happens with the mustard seeds and the leaven, even though you can't see it now. In that sense, I think we have to disregard quantitative measures of success. After all, we're not a business operation that can look at the numbers to measure whether our policy has been successful and whether we're selling more and more. Rather, we're performing a service, and in the end, when we've done our job, we put it in the Lord's hands. On the other hand, this doesn't mean that everything is totally in vain. In fact, there are stirrings of faith among young people on every continent.

Perhaps the time has come to say farewell to the idea of traditionally Catholic cultures. Maybe we are facing a new and different kind of epoch in the Church's history, where Christianity will again be characterized more by the mustard seed, where it will exist in small, seemingly insignificant groups that nonetheless live an intensive struggle against evil and bring the good into the world—that let God in. I see that there is once more a great deal of activity of this kind. I don't want to cite any individual examples here. There are certainly no mass conversions to Christianity, no reversal of the historical paradigm, no about-face. But there are powerful ways in which faith is present, inspiring people again and giving them dynamism and joy. In other words, there is a presence of faith that means something for the world.

All the same, more and more people are asking themselves whether the ship of the Church will still be sailing at all in the future. Is it still worthwhile to get on board?

Yes, I firmly believe that it is. It is a well-tried, yet youthful ship. The very diagnosis of the present makes it all the more clear that we need it. Just try to imagine for a moment the current parallelogram of forces without this ship; you'll see what a collapse there would be if it were absent, what a precipitous fall in spiritual energy.

One can also see, in fact, that the decline of the Church and of Christianity that we have lived through in the last thirty or forty years is partially to blame for the spiritual breakdowns, the disorientation, the demoralization that we are witnessing. In that respect, I would say that if the ship didn't already exist, it would be necessary to invent it. It corresponds to such deep human needs, it is so deeply anchored in what man is and needs and is meant to be, that there is also a guarantee in man that the ship won't simply sink, because man will never, as I believe, lose his essential powers.

For the time being, it is hard to imagine that a life according to the Catholic faith might come to be regarded once more in the foreseeable future as particularly modern, even though, looked at more closely, it is possibly the most alternative, most self-confident, and most radical way of living that can be conceived of today.

People think they know the Church. They think she is a very ancient system that has become sclerotic over time, that gets progressively more insulated and rigid, that forms a sort of armor that smothers one's personal life. That is the impression of many people. Few people manage to recognize instead that there is something fresh and also bold and large-minded here, something that offers escape from the stale habits of one's life. But precisely those who have gone through the experience of modernity see this.

It's evident that people also no longer know what the Church actually is and is supposed to be. The true significance of the signs and words of this faith are hidden behind a kind of fog bank. When it comes to Zen Buddhism, to take an example, it would never occur to anyone that he could understand this entity so easily without teaching and effort.

An awareness needs to develop that in fact to a large extent we no longer know Christianity at all. For example, how many images in a church no longer say anything to some people? The original meaning is no longer generally understood. Even terms that are still barely familiar to the middle generation, like tabernacle and so forth, have become foreign words. Nevertheless, the predominant mentality is still that we already know all about Christianity and are now in search of something different.

There needs to be a renewal of what you could call a curiosity about Christianity, the desire really to discover what it's all about. It would be very important for preachers to show the way out of this feeling of staleness, this feeling that we are already long familiar with this, to create curiosity about the richness hidden in Christianity, so that this richness is regarded, no longer as a matter of burdensome systems, but as a living treasure that it is worth knowing.

Let me briefly anticipate this important question: What exactly does "Catholic" mean? Is it a certain system? Is it a certain way of ordering the world and things? In your writings I've found the following statement: "All men are creatures of the one God and are therefore of equal rank; all are related to one another as brothers and sisters, all are responsible for one another, and all are summoned to love their neighbor, whoever he may be." Is that a truly Catholic sentence?

Yes, I hope so. Faith in God as creator is right at the heart of what is Catholic. From this faith derives belief in the unity of humanity in all men and in the equality of human dignity.

Now, I have my doubts as to whether the quintessentially Catholic, as a living structure, can be captured in a formula. One can try to indicate the essential elements, but it requires more than just knowing something about it, as I can, for example, know something about a party program. It is an entrance into a living structure, and it comprises the totality of one's life plan. For this reason, it can never, I think, be expressed in words alone. It has to be a way of living, of lived identification, a merging with a way of thinking and understanding. The two things enrich each other.

Of course, it is possible to specify crucial points, namely, that in the first place we believe in God, and a God who knows man, who enters into relation with men, and who is accessible to us, has become accessible in Christ, and who makes history with us. Who has become so concrete to us that he has also founded a community.

But I would say that all of this becomes understandable only when one sets off on the way. Thinking and living belong together; otherwise there is, I believe, no understanding of the Catholic reality.

There is evidently no formula for it, but can one at least say what belongs to the substance of this faith?

To the substance of the faith belongs the fact that we look upon Christ as the living, incarnate Son of God made man; that because of him we believe in God, the triune God, the Creator of heaven and earth; that we believe that this God bends so far down, can become so small, that he is concerned about man and has created history with man, a history whose vessel, whose privileged place of expression, is the Church. In this connection, the Church is not a merely human institution—though it is impossible to ignore that she is full of human elements. Being with and in the Church belongs to the faith, and in this Church the Holy Scriptures can be both lived and appropriated.

"Whoever can be as small as this child", it says in the New Testament in Matthew, "is the greatest in the kingdom of heaven."

The theology of littleness is a basic category of Christianity. After all, the tenor of our faith is that God's distinctive greatness is revealed precisely in powerlessness. That in the long run, the strength of history is precisely in those who *love*, which is to say, in a strength that, properly speaking, cannot be measured according to categories of power. So in order to show who he is, God consciously revealed himself in the powerlessness of Nazareth and Golgotha. Thus, it is not the one who can destroy the most who is the most powerful—in the world, of course, destructive capacity is still the real proof of power—but, on the contrary, the least power of love is already greater than the greatest power of destruction.

You once said that Christian faith is not a theory but an event.

And that's very important. What's essential about Christ himself is not that he proclaimed certain ideas—which, of course, he also did. Rather, I become a Christian by believing in this event. God stepped into the world and acted; so it is an action, a reality, not only an intellectual entity.

What is the most fascinating thing about being Catholic for you personally?

The fascinating thing is this great living history into which we enter. Looked at in purely human terms, it is something

extraordinary. That an institution with so many human weaknesses and failures is nonetheless preserved in its continuity
and that I, living within this great communion, can know
that I am in communion with all the living and the dead; and
that I also find in it a certainty about the essence of my life—
namely, God who has turned to me—on which I can found
my life, with which I can live and die.

*Aren't Jesus Christ and, with him, the whole design of the Church
mysteries in themselves that one must either accept or reject, "take it
or leave it", as the Americans say?*

To be sure, one must decide. That is correct. But not in the
same way that I can, for example, take or not take a cup of
coffee. The decision goes deeper. It affects the whole structure of my life; it affects me in the core of my being. If I do
my best to construct my life without or *against* God, then it's
obviously going to turn out differently than if I direct it toward God. It is a decision that encompasses the whole direction of my own existence as such: how I look at the world,
how I myself want to be and will be. It is not one of the many
casual decisions in the market of available possibilities. Here,
on the contrary, the *whole* plan of my life is at issue.

*Many see religion mainly as a sort of spiritual corset, an aid, a device,
that a weak, ignorant person contrives in order to cope with himself
and the world. As the psychoanalyst C. G. Jung expressed it: "Religions are psychotherapeutic systems in the strictest sense of the word.
The Church has powerful images that express the scope of the problem of the psyche." Is this sufficient? Is this by itself faith?*

What Jung says, and what Drewermann, for that matter, has
picked up, is correct, namely, that religion does have healing

power and does answer primal needs and anxieties and does help to manage them. However, if religion is regarded only as a psychotherapeutic trick, or is reduced to a self-healing with images, then it no longer works. For in that case we ultimately see through the untruth of these images, and they lose their healing power.

This is certainly an added bonus of religion, but it is not its true essence. It is something more, and this appears also in the fact that in all its phases (and also without any help from psychotherapy) mankind simply cannot do otherwise than reach out toward the eternal, the wholly other, and try to enter into relation with it.

The essence of religion is the relation of man beyond himself to the unknown reality that faith calls God. It is man's capacity to go beyond all tangible, measurable reality and to enter into this primordial relation. Man lives in relationships, and the ultimate goodness of his life depends on the rightness of his essential relationships—I mean father, mother, brother and sister, and so forth—the basic relationships that are inscribed in his being. But none of these relationships can be right if the first relationship, the relationship with God, is not right. This relationship itself, I would say, is, properly speaking, the content of religion.

All the great cultures we know of had or have religion as the most important thing in common. It seems that there is a sort of unison of doctrines, for example, in the exhortation to moderation, the warning against egotism and autonomy. So then why shouldn't all religions be the same? Why should the God of the Christians be better than, say, the God of the Indians? And why should there be only one religion that confers true bliss?

This proposal, which has been made since the early days of the science of comparative religions in the Enlightenment (though it had come up even before that), is already self-contradictory with respect to the religions themselves, for these are plainly not the same. There are various levels [of religion], and there are religions that are obviously sick, religions that can also be destructive for man.

The Marxist critique of religion is correct insofar as there are religions and religious practices that alienate man from himself. As an example, let us think of the fact that in Africa belief in spirits continues to be a great obstacle to the development of the land and to the construction of a modern economic organization. If I constantly have to protect myself against spirits, and an irrational fear governs my whole sense of life, then I am not rightly living what religion at its depth should be. And so we can also see that in the Indian religious cosmos ("Hinduism" is a rather misleading designation for a multiplicity of religions) there are very different forms: very high and pure ones that are marked by the idea of love, but also wholly gruesome ones that include ritual murder.

We know that human sacrifices shape a portion of the history of religion in a terrible way; we know that political religion has become an instrument of destruction and oppression; there are, as we know, pathologies in the Christian religion itself. Witch burning was a recrudescence of Germanic customs. It had, with difficulty, been overcome by the early medieval missionaries, and then it reemerged in the late Middle Ages as faith began to grow weak. In a word, even the gods are not all alike; there are decidedly negative divine figures, whether we think of the Greek or, for example, the Indian religious cosmos. The idea that all religions are equal is already disproved by the simple fact of the history of religion.

But could we not also accept that someone can be saved through a faith other than the Catholic?

That's a different question altogether. It is definitely possible for someone to receive from his religion directives that help him become a pure person, which also, if we want to use the word, help him to please God and reach salvation. This is not at all excluded by what I said; on the contrary, this undoubtedly happens on a large scale. It is just that it would be misguided to deduce from this fact that the religions themselves all stand in simple equality to one another, as in one big concert, one big symphony in which ultimately all mean the same thing.

Religions can also make it harder for man to be good. This can happen even in Christianity because of false ways of living the Christian reality, sectarian deformations, and so forth. In this sense, in the history and universe of religions, there is always a great necessity to purify religion so that it does not become an obstacle to the right relation to God but in fact puts man on the right path.

I would say that if Christianity, appealing to the figure of Christ, has claimed to be the true religion among the religions of history, this means [in connection with what I just said] that in the figure of Christ the truly purifying power has appeared out of the Word of God. Christians do not necessarily always live this power well and as they should, but it furnishes the criterion and the orientation for the purifications that are indispensable for keeping religion from becoming a system of oppression and alienation, so that it may really become a way for man to God and to himself.

Many think, however, that precisely the Christian-Catholic religion is the expression of a pessimistic world view.

The French Revolution saw the birth of the ideology according to which Christianity, because it believes in the end of the world, in judgment, and the like, is by nature pessimistic, whereas modernity, which has discovered progress as the law of history, is by nature optimistic. We now see that these comparisons are slowly dissolving. We see the self-confidence of modernity increasingly crumble. For it is becoming clearer and clearer that progress also involves progress in the powers of destruction, that ethically man is not equal to his own reason, and that his capability can become a capability to destroy. Christianity in fact does not have such a notion that history necessarily always progresses, that, in other words, essentially things are always getting better for mankind.

When we read the Book of Revelation, we see that humanity actually moves in circles. Over and over there are horrors that then dissipate, only to be followed by new ones. Nor is there any prophecy of an inner-historical, man-made state of salvation. The idea that human affairs necessarily get better and better has no support in the Christian outlook. What does, on the other hand, belong to the Christian faith is the certainty that God never abandons man and that man therefore can never become a pure failure, even though today many believe it would be better if man had never appeared on the scene.

In this sense, the categories of optimism and pessimism are simply out of place. The Christian can see, as can any reasonable man, that there can be great crises in history, that perhaps such crises await us even today as well. He can also recognize that history does not develop in a positive direction by some internal automatic reflex; in other words, that there are very real perils. However, he has the final optimism that God holds the world in his hands and that even fearsome atrocities such as Auschwitz, which ought to shake us to the core, are held firmly in check by the fact that in spite of everything God is stronger than evil.

The Cross—a ghastly symbol?

In one respect, of course, the Cross does have a terrible aspect that we ought not to remove. It was, as a matter of fact, the cruelest form of execution known to antiquity. It could not be used on Romans, because that would have stained the honor of Rome, so to speak. To see that the purest of men, who was more than a man, was executed in such a grisly way can make us frightened of ourselves. But we also need to be frightened of ourselves and out of our self-complacency. Here, I think, Luther was right when he said that man must first be frightened of himself so that he can then find the right way.

However, the Cross doesn't stop at being a horror; it is not merely a horror, because the one who looks down at us from the Cross is not a failure, a desperate man, not one of the horrible victims of humanity. For this crucified man says something different from Spartacus and his failed adherents, because, after all, what looks down at us from this Cross is a goodness that enables a new beginning in the midst of life's horror. The goodness of God himself looks on us, God who surrenders himself into our hands, delivers himself to us, and bears the whole horror of history with us. Looked at more deeply, this sign, which forces us to look at the dangerousness of man and all his heinous deeds, at the same time makes us look upon God, who is stronger, stronger in his weakness, and upon the fact that we are loved by God. It is in this sense a sign of forgiveness that also brings hope into the abysses of history.

It is indeed often asked today how we can still speak of God and do theology after Auschwitz. I would say that the

Cross recapitulates in advance the horror of Auschwitz. God is crucified and says to us that this God who is apparently so weak is the God who incomprehensibly forgives us and who in his seeming absence is stronger.

The truth about man and God often seems sad and hard. Is faith naturally something only stronger constitutions can take? After all, it's often felt as an unreasonable claim. How is joy in faith to arise?

I would put it the other way around: faith gives joy. When God is not there, the world becomes desolate, and everything becomes boring, and everything is completely unsatisfactory. It's easy to see today how a world empty of God is also increasingly consuming itself, how it has become a wholly joyless world. The great joy comes from the fact that there is this great love, and that is the essential message of faith. You are unswervingly loved. This also explains why Christianity spread first predominantly among the weak and suffering.

To be sure, we can interpret that in a Marxist way and say, it was only a consolation instead of revolution. But I believe that we are in a certain sense beyond these slogans. In those days, Christianity brought masters and slaves to one another in a new way, so that already Paul could say to a master: Don't harm your slave, for he has become your brother.

To that extent it can be said that the basic element of Christianity is joy. Joy not in the sense of cheap fun, which can conceal desperation in the background. We know, in fact, that slapstick comedy often masks desperation. Rather, it is joy in the proper sense. A joy that exists together with a difficult life and also makes this life liveable. The history of Jesus Christ begins, according to the Gospel, with the angel saying to Mary, "Rejoice!" On the night of the nativity the angels say again: We proclaim to you a great joy. And Jesus says, "I proclaim to you the good news." So the heart of the matter is always expressed in these terms: I proclaim to you a great joy, God is here, you are beloved, and this stands firm forever.

Yet it seems generally easier not to believe than to believe. It is paradoxical: on the one hand, faith is present in principle, man is a religious being; on the other hand, he has to struggle with it constantly.

The ease of unbelief is nonetheless relative. It exists in the sense that it is easy to throw off the bonds of faith and to say, I am not going to exert myself; this is burdensome; I'm leaving that aside. This first stage is what you might call the easy part of unbelief. But to live with this is not at all so easy. To live without faith means, then, to find oneself first in some sort of nihilistic state and then, nonetheless, to search for reference points. Living a life of unbelief has its complications. If you examine the philosophy of unbelief in Sartre, Camus, and so forth, you see that readily.

The act of faith, as new start and acceptance, may be complicated, although at the moment when faith really hits me—"you may rejoice"—it has in turn its great interim ease. So we mustn't unilaterally emphasize the toil. The ease of unbelief and the difficulty of belief lie on different planes. Unbelief, too, is a heavy burden, and in my opinion even more so than faith is. Faith also makes man light. This can be seen in the Church Fathers, especially in monastic theology. To believe means that we become like angels, they say. We can fly, because we no longer weigh so heavy in our own estimation. To become a believer means to become light, to escape our own gravity, which drags us down, and thus to enter the weightlessness of faith.

How is a good Catholic different from other people?

Catholics are human beings like everyone else. Among Catholics there is every degree of good and evil—just as, conversely, in all religions there are men of interior purity [*Lauterkeit*] who through their myths somehow touch the great mystery and find the right way of being human. I think that we shouldn't try to calculate where the best men are. One thing, however, we do dare to say: Whoever lives the faith in real patience and lets himself be formed by it is purified through many setbacks and weaknesses.

Is the Catholic happier than others?

Happiness is, of course, a multifaceted category. Just think of the fact that the Sermon on the Mount begins with the so-called Beatitudes. The Lord opens what you might call a school of happiness; he presents Christianity to humanity as a school of happiness: "I will show you the way." But if one looks again, this school of happiness contradicts what men customarily understand by happiness.

We would say that the happy man is the one who has sufficient possessions. Who has the means to be able to shape a nice life for himself. We would say that someone who is cheerful and who succeeds at everything in life is happy. *He* says: Blessed are those who mourn. This means, in other words, that his doctrine of happiness is very paradoxical, at least compared with what we understand by that term. It is not happiness in the sense of comfort. In this respect, one can grasp quite well what conversion means. One must relinquish the customary criteria—"happiness is wealth, possession, power." For precisely when one makes these things the measure, one is on the wrong path. So Catholics are not promised an "exterior" happiness but rather a deep interior security [*Geborgensein*] through communion with the Lord. That *He* is an ultimate light of happiness in one's life is in fact a part of all this.

But where is God, where does one find him? Does he keep himself hidden? It does seem that God reveals himself very, very rarely. People are in despair because they think that he doesn't speak to them, he gives no signs, he doesn't send any signals.

He doesn't do so loudly, he doesn't necessarily do so in forms such as natural catastrophes—although he can speak to us through these—he doesn't do so, as I was saying, in a loud voice. Yet he does do so again and again. To be sure, it is also important for the receiver, so to speak, to be tuned to the broadcaster. And our average way of living and thinking causes too much interference that keeps the sound from coming through. Moreover, we are so alienated from his voice that we simply do not recognize it immediately as his. But I would still say that everyone who is in some sense attentive can experience and sense for himself that now *He* is speaking to me. And it is a chance for me to get to know him. Precisely in catastrophic situations he can suddenly break in, if I am awake and if someone helps me decipher the message. Of course, he does not speak loudly, but he speaks through signs and through events in our life, through our fellowmen. A little bit of vigilance is certainly called for as well, and it is also necessary that we not get wholly caught up in what is superficial.

Are Catholics allowed to doubt, or, if they do, are they hypocrites and heretics? The strange thing about Christians seems to be that they distinguish between religious and scientific truth. They study Darwin and go to church. Is such a division possible in the first place? There can, after all, be only one truth: either the world was really created in six days, or it developed over millions of years.

In a world as confused as ours, doubt will inevitably assail individuals again and again. Doubt need not be immediately associated with a fall from faith. I can sincerely take up the questions that press upon me while holding fast to God, holding to the essential core of faith. On the one hand, I can try to find solutions for the seeming contradictions. On the other hand, I can also be confident that, though I can't find them all, there are solutions even when I can't find them. Again and again in the history of theology, too, there are things that remain unresolved for the moment that should not be explained away by forced interpretations.

Part of faith is also the patience of time. The theme you have just mentioned—Darwin, creation, the theory of evolution—is the subject of a dialogue that is not yet finished and, with our present means, is probably also impossible to settle at the moment. Not that the problem of the six days is a particularly urgent issue between faith and modern scientific research into the origin of the world. For it is obvious even in the Bible that this is a theological framework and is not intended simply to recount the history of creation. In the Old Testament itself there are other accounts of creation. In the Book of Job and in the Wisdom literature we have creation narratives that make it clear that even then believers themselves did not think that the creation account was, so to speak, a photographic depiction of the process of creation. It only seeks to convey a glimpse of the essential truth, namely, that the world comes from the power of God and is his creation. How the processes actually occurred is a wholly different question, which even the Bible itself leaves wide open. Conversely, I think that in great measure the theory of evolution has not gotten beyond hypotheses and is often mixed with almost mythical philosophies that have yet to be critically discussed.

Many are not able to make the jump from childhood faith to adult faith. How can someone who has read the biblical critics find his way back to pure faith?

He must learn that the complicated history of the genesis of biblical texts does not affect the faith as such. What shines through this history is something different and greater. Through this complicated historical genesis, which, by the way, is also always hypothetical, one can see, on the contrary, how statements and realities, which are not simply invented by man, impress themselves upon his consciousness. I believe that precisely when one comes to know the human factors of biblical history, one also sees all the more clearly that it is not just a case of human factors, but that another is speaking here. Consequently, one can leave to scholarship the whole range of technical issues concerning how this sort of thing works. Scholarship for its part gives us elucidations that help us return to the simple act of faith, precisely faith in the fact that not just men have been the builders in this wholly unique history but that something greater happened in it.

How many ways are there to God?

As many as there are people. For even within the same faith each man's way is an entirely personal one. We have Christ's word: I am the way. In that respect, there is ultimately one way, and everyone who is on the way to God is therefore in some sense also on the way of Jesus Christ. But this does not mean that all ways are identical in terms of consciousness and will, but, on the contrary, the one way is so big that it becomes a personal way for each man.

Tertullian gave us the paradox "I believe because it is absurd." Au-

gustine believed "in order to understand". Why does Cardinal Rat-
zinger believe?

I am a decided Augustinian. Just as creation comes from reason and is reasonable, faith is, so to speak, the fulfillment of
creation and thus the door to understanding. I am convinced
of that. Faith therefore is access to understanding and knowing. Tertullian's remark—he loves exaggerated formulations—naturally reflects the sum of his thinking in general.
He wanted to say that God shows himself precisely in a paradoxical relation to what prevails in the world. And in doing
this God shows his divinity. But Tertullian was admittedly
somewhat hostile to philosophy. In that respect I don't share
his position but that of Saint Augustine.

Have you also developed something like your own expression for the
core of the faith?

I don't need any new motto here. It seems to me that
Augustine's statement, which Thomas, too, later adopted, really describes the right direction. I believe! And already the
act of faith itself implies that this comes from him who is reason itself. And in first submitting myself in faith to him,
whom I do not understand, I know that by this very act I am
opening the door to understanding.

Most people in our time cannot believe what they know and do not
know what they should believe. Now you yourself combine a unity
and integration of thought and faith that is no longer familiar to us
skeptical and errant moderns. How does it feel to live like that?

I don't dare judge here whether all modern men in general
really lack this inner unity, or whether they don't in fact find

unity in many ways. Every man is inwardly pulled between many poles, and this is, of course, true for me and for any priest and bishop. For one's interests, talents and handicaps, knowledge and ignorance, the faith of the Church as a whole, do not coincide automatically. In this sense, there is in every man, including me, an inner tension. But I wouldn't describe it as an internal division. Believing with the Church and knowing that I may entrust myself to this knowledge and knowing that the other things I know receive light from it and, conversely, can deepen it—that does hold me together. Above all, the foundational act of faith in Christ, and the attempt to bring one's life into unity in terms of that faith, unifies the tensions, so that they do not become a fissure, a fracture.

In connection with the new evangelization you have spoken of new encounters, indeed, of the necessity of a Christian revolution. For, as you put it, it is not subtle studies that bring forth "the vital new cultural forms of Christianity". Rather, it is necessary to reacquaint men with Jesus. It seems to me that many more people today would very much like to believe—if only they could. It no longer seems so easy as it once was.

That is plain. We now have so much knowledge, so many experiences, and, on the other hand, we find that faith has been so elaborated upon and oversystematized that access is no longer so easy to come by. I do think that we need a sort of revolution of faith in many senses. First of all, we need it in the sense of courage even to contradict commonly held convictions. There is, in fact, today among most people a certain average ideology whose drift is as follows: Everyone has to achieve a certain standard of living; everyone has to be able to realize himself by satisfying his desires and wishes; and, when all is said and done, in all of this God is an unknown quantity that does not really count. In keeping with this, morality tends to be rather a product of chance and of the calculation of happiness.

As I said, the average ideology in which we live today and which forces itself on us day by day entices us to accept convictions that basically insulate man from the essential. On the one hand, then, he can no longer penetrate into what is essential, but he notices, on the other hand, that he lacks something. For the great collective pathologies that we have today rest upon the fact that there is some deficit in man's life and that he perceives a lack. In this sense, we ought to have the courage to rise up against what is regarded as "normal" for a person at the end of the twentieth century and to rediscover faith in its simplicity.

This discovery could consist quite simply in an encounter with Christ, which, however, is not an encounter with a historical hero but with God who is man. And only when this truly penetrates into a life does life get a different orientation. When this happens, a culture of faith also arises. I am convinced of that. The important point is that a decision like this is never purely individualistic but that it is communicated, that it forms community. And in the measure in which it is lived, it forms a life-style and also produces culture.

Many people feverishly await the future. In many cases a downright hysteria about the future, filled with feverish expectations, has arisen. Never before has so much been coming to a close, so much beginning. Occasionally, one may have the impression that, yes, much is also developing in a positive direction but that, on the other hand, this world, as it is, is also a great madhouse. A world in which a society of pleasure and luxury exists next to growing poverty, a world of wars, of natural catastrophes that visit us more and more frequently, not to mention a world in which there are clear signs of cultural decline, in which there are great losses in insight and wisdom. Never before have there been so many unstable people, so many addicts, so many broken relationships, troubled children, misery—and, paradoxically, the demoralization of an affluent society.

Cardinal Ratzinger, you once said that what our time is lacking is not so much the capacity to mourn as the capacity to rejoice. But is it not also becoming increasingly hard for a person to rejoice?

Something I constantly notice is that unembarrassed joy has become rarer. Joy today is increasingly saddled with moral and ideological burdens, so to speak. When someone rejoices, he is afraid of offending against solidarity with the many people who suffer. I don't have any right to rejoice, people think, in a world where there is so much misery, so much injustice.

I can understand that. There is a moral attitude at work here. But this attitude is nonetheless wrong. The loss of joy does not make the world better—and, conversely, refusing joy for the sake of suffering does not help those who suffer. The contrary is true. The world needs people who discover the good, who rejoice in it and thereby derive the impetus and courage to do good. Joy, then, does not break with solidarity. When it is the right kind of joy, when it is not egotistic, when it comes from the perception of the good, then it wants to communicate itself, and it gets passed on. In this connection, it always strikes me that in the poor neighborhoods of, say, South America, one sees many more laughing, happy people than among us. Obviously, despite all their misery, they still have the perception of the good to which they cling and in which they can find encouragement and strength.

In this sense we have a new need for that primordial trust which ultimately only faith can give. That the world is basically good, that God is there and is good. That it is good to live and to be a human being. This results, then, in the courage to rejoice, which in turn becomes commitment to making sure that other people, too, can rejoice and receive good news.

A word now on the two faces of our present day, as you have described them. There is a new awareness of solidarity, of responsibility for humanity as a whole, of responsibility for creation. There are movements toward unification and a desire for solidarity to aid people in crisis situations, to promote peace and overcome misery. That is one thing a citizen of this decade sees and should be grateful for. It is also a very practical indication that the good in man cannot be crushed.

On the other hand, you have spoken of the great madhouse and of horrendous demoralization. We all see that. I believe that here mass society as well as the possibilities that have arisen through the technical domination of the world have created new dimensions of evil. This cannot be overlooked.

It is a great challenge both to combat this loss of individuality, which at the same time isolates man and drives him into radical solitude, and to create wholesome social opportunities. These challenges call for our complete commitment, but they cannot be satisfied merely through technology, through our own efforts and activity.

I would say that two things emerge here: the fact that man is a moral being who has responsibility for himself and for the totality of mankind, but the fact, too, that he is also a being who can obtain the resources to go on only from God.

PART I

Personal Biography

Background and Vocation

Your Eminence, what do you think of this idea: We come into this world and what we want to know, we already know, and where we want to be, we already are?

That is going too far, to my mind. I don't know now where that statement comes from, but man comes into the world as a questioner. Aristotle even says—and Thomas Aquinas says it too—as a *tabula rasa*. In other words, they contest that men have innate knowledge; for them the mind begins as pure readiness to receive. I would nuance that a bit. But at any rate it is correct that man exists first as a questioner, who, however, is, so to speak, open from within to the answers.

To a certain extent I am a Platonist. I think that a kind of memory, of recollection of God, is, as it were, etched in man, though it needs to be awakened. Man doesn't simply know what he is supposed to know, nor is he simply there, but is a man, a being on the way.

Precisely the biblical religion of the Old and New Testament always strongly accentuated the image of the wandering people of God, which in the case of Israel really was a wandering people. This image exemplifies the nature of human existence as such. That man is a being under way and that his way is not a fiction, but that something really happens to him in this life, and that he can seek, can find, but can also miss the mark.

You often use the word "providence". What meaning does it have for you?

I am quite firmly convinced that God really sees us and that he leaves us freedom—and nevertheless leads us. I can often see that things which at first seemed irksome, dangerous, unpleasant, somehow at some point come together. Suddenly one realizes that it was good thus, that this was the right way. For me this means in a very practical way that my life is not made up of chance occurrences but that someone foresees and also, so to speak, precedes me, whose thinking precedes mine and who prepares my life. I can refuse this, but I can also accept it, and then I realize that I am really guided by a providential light.

Now this does not mean that man is completely determined but rather that what is preordained calls forth precisely man's freedom. Just as we hear in the story of the talents. Five are given; and the one who receives them has a definite task, but he can do it in this way or that. At any rate, he has his mission, his particular gift. No one is superfluous, no one is in vain, everyone must try to recognize what his life's call is and how he can best live up to the call that is waiting for him.

You were born on April 16, 1927, in Marktl am Inn in Upper Bavaria. You were born on a Holy Saturday. Does that suit you?

Yes, I'm pleased to have been born on the vigil of Easter, already on the way to Easter, but not yet there, for it is still veiled. I find that a very good day, which in some sense hints at my conception of history and my own situation: on the threshold of Easter, but not yet through the door.

Your parents were named Mary and Joseph. You were baptized just four hours after your birth, at 8:30 in the morning. They say it was a stormy day.

Needless to say, I have no recollection of that. My brother and sister have told me that there was a lot of snow, that it was very cold, although it was April 16. But that is nothing extraordinary in Bavaria.

Still, it is uncommon to be baptized just four hours after being born.

That is true. But that has to do with the fact—and this is certainly something that I'm pleased by—that it was Holy Saturday. The Easter Vigil was not yet celebrated in those days, so that the Resurrection was celebrated in the morning, with the blessing of the water, which then served throughout the whole year as baptismal water. And because the baptismal liturgy was consequently taking place in the Church, my parents said: "Well, the boy's already here", so it is natural that he be baptized too at this liturgical point in time, which is the time when the Church baptizes. And the coincidence that I was born at the very moment when the Church was preparing her baptismal water, so that I was the first person baptized with the new water, does indeed mean something to me. Because it situates me particularly in the context of Easter and also binds birth and baptism in a very suggestive way.

You grew up in the country as the youngest of three children. Your father was a constable, the family poor rather than well-off. Your mother, you once recounted, even made her own soap.

My parents had married late, and a Bavarian constable of my father's rank—he was a simple commissioner—was modestly paid. We were not poor in the strict sense of the word, because the monthly salary was guaranteed, but we did have to live very frugally and simply, for which I am very grateful. For thereby joys are made possible that one cannot have in wealth. I often think back on how wonderful it was that we could be happy over the smallest things and how we also tried to do things for one another. How this very modest, sometimes financially difficult situation gave rise to an inner solidarity that bound us deeply together.

Our parents naturally had to make tremendous sacrifices so that all three of us could study. We recognized this and tried to respond. In this way, this climate of great simplicity was a source of much joy as well as love for one another. We realized how much was given to us and how much our parents took upon themselves.

The business about the soap needs some explanation. It wasn't due to poverty but to the wartime situation in which one had to find some way to obtain goods that were not available in sufficient quantities. Our mother was by profession a cook and had many talents, and she knew such recipes by heart. With her great imagination and her practical skill she always knew, at the very moment when there was hunger in the land, how to conjure up a good meal out of the simplest and scantiest means.

My mother was very warm-hearted and had great inner strength; my father was more markedly rationalistic and deliberate. He was a reflective believer. He always understood clearly at the outset what was going on and always had an astonishingly accurate judgment. When Hitler came to power, he said: There's going to be war, now we need a house.

There was a Georg Ratzinger who played a certain role in Bavarian history.

He was a great-uncle of mine, my father's uncle. He was a priest and had a doctorate in theology. As a representative in the state and national assemblies, he was really a champion of the rights of the peasants and of the simple people in general. He fought—I've read this in the minutes of the state parliament—against child labor, which at that time was still considered a scandalous, impudent position to take. He was obviously a tough man. His achievements and his political standing also made everyone proud of him.

What were things like at your house? How did you live?

First of all, there was a good deal of moving around connected with my father's job as a constable. I have no personal recollection of my place of birth, Marktl. We moved away when I was two years old. After that we were in Tittmoning, where the constabulary was quartered in what had formerly been the house of a cathedral provost. The house was very nice, but it was extremely uncomfortable to live in. The former chapter room was our bedroom, whereas the other rooms were very small. We had sufficient space. But we also realized, of course, that it was an old, dilapidated house. For my mother, it was really awful. Every day she had to drag wood and coal up two long flights of stairs. Later, in Aschau, we lived in a very pretty villa that a farmer had built for himself and rented to the constabulary. Compared with today's amenities, even that house was quite simple. There was no bath. But there was running water.

With an eye to his retirement, my father bought an old, likewise very simple farmhouse in Hufschlag near Traunstein. Instead of tap water, there was a well, which was very picturesque. On one side of the house there was an oak forest interspersed with beeches, on the other side were the mountains, and when we opened our eyes in the morning, the first thing we could see was the mountains. In the front we had apple trees, plum trees, and a lot of flowers that my mother had cultivated in the garden. It was a beautiful, large plot of ground —in terms of location it was heavenly. And in the old barns you could have the most marvelous dreams and play wonderful games.

It was an unexplored world. At bottom, it was impossible to discover everything about it, because it was so varied. There was an old weaving room in the house, because the previous owners had to all appearances been weavers. The rooms themselves were of the greatest simplicity, and the house—I believe it had been built in 1726—was on the whole in great need of repairs. The rain came in and so forth. But it was simply wonderful; it was a childhood dream. We felt altogether happy there even without comforts. For my father, who had to pay for the necessary repairs, for my mother, who carried water from the well, it was perhaps less fun. But we experienced it as a real paradise. It took us just under half an hour to get to the city. But even that—the fact that you were on the move like that—was wonderful. So we didn't feel at all the lack of modern amenities but experienced the adventure, freedom, and beauty of an old house with its inner warmth.

Was it strict in your parents' house?

In a certain sense it was. My father was a very upright and also a very strict man. But we always sensed the goodness behind his strictness. And for that reason we could basically accept his strictness without trouble. From the very beginning my mother always compensated for my father's perhaps excessive strictness by her warmth and kindness. They had two very different temperaments, and this difference was also exactly what made them complementary. Yes, I have to say that it was strict, but there was still a lot of warmth and kindness and joy. That was augmented by the fact that we played with one another, even our parents joined in, and that music also had a bigger and bigger role in our family life. Music, after all, has the power to bring people together.

You are a great lover of Mozart.

Yes! Although we moved around a very great deal in my childhood, the family basically always remained in the area between the Inn and the Salzach. And the largest and most important and best part of my youth I spent in Traunstein, which very much reflects the influence of Salzburg. You might say that there Mozart thoroughly penetrated our souls, and his music still touches me very deeply, because it is so luminous and yet at the same time so deep. His music is by no means just entertainment; it contains the whole tragedy of human existence.

Yes, art is elemental. Reason alone as it's expressed in the sciences can't be man's complete answer to reality, and it can't express everything that man can, wants to, and has to express. I think God built this into man. Art along with science is the highest gift God has given him.

Your parents sent all three children to boarding school. How did that come about?

At that time it was the only way to get a better education. There were very few high schools [*Gymnasien*] in the country. Since the schools were so far away, there was generally no other choice but boarding school. My sister attended a high school [*Mittelschule*] run by the Franciscan Sisters. She rode there on her bicycle; it was five kilometers away, and she continued to live at home. She herself then asked to stay at the boarding school and was allowed to. My brother was the first to go to the *Gymnasium*, which meant boarding school. There was simply no other way. At first I went to school every day from home. After two years, now that I was the only child at home, the idea came up that it would be a good supplement to my education if I also went to boarding school. And it certainly had—it wasn't easy for me, I must say—a good corrective function. You learn a different kind of social interaction and also how to fit in. This lasted only two years, however, for all the boarding schools in Traunstein ended up being converted into military hospitals. So, from that point on I was back home.

Could one say that the family home was markedly religious?

One could certainly say that. My father was a very religious man. On Sundays he went to Mass at six, then to the main liturgy at nine, and again in the afternoon. My mother had a very warm and heartfelt piety. On that point the two, again, were at one in different ways. Religion was quite central.

What was your religious education at home like? I mean, a lot of parents today clearly have a problem with it.

Religion was a part of life. The simple fact of praying together made it so. There was prayer at all meals. Whenever our school schedule would allow it, we naturally also went to daily Mass, and on Sundays we went to church together. Later, when my father was retired, we generally also prayed the rosary; for the rest my parents relied on the catechesis we received in school. My father also bought us things to read; there were magazines, for example, when we made our First Holy Communion. But there wasn't explicit religious education; it was given by family prayer and church attendance.

As a young person, what did you find so fascinating about the faith?

From the very beginning—it was exactly the same for my brother and sister, I think—I had a lot of interest in the liturgy. My parents had already bought me my first missal when I was in the second grade. It was actually terribly exciting to penetrate into the mysterious world of the Latin liturgy and to find out what was actually happening, what it meant, what was being said. And so then we progressed by degrees from a children's missal to a more complete missal, to the complete version. That was a kind of voyage of discovery.

What is a missal?

A missal is the book that the priest uses at the altar for Mass. There are smaller versions—and in translation—that the ordinary Christian can obtain.

Then we found the liturgical feasts fascinating, of course, with the music and all the ornamentation and images. That is one aspect. The other is that from the very beginning everything that was said in religion interested me intellectually as well. You could say that I was led on step by step in my own thinking. In addition, it was a definite advantage that in the Nazi era you had to explain yourself accurately. Everyone knew: he is Catholic, he goes to church, or even wants to be a priest. In this way you got drawn into controversies and had to learn to arm yourself. It was obviously interesting to find arguments and to understand them, so that it also became an intellectual adventure, which, so to speak, opened wider and wider and revealed broader horizons. This combination of the festive-liturgical and the intellectual seemed to me, as I sought to understand the world, an especially wonderful opportunity for enriching one's life.

There is obviously a powerful connection here with your Bavarian homeland as well as with distinctively Bavarian Catholicism. You have repeatedly stressed that you want to defend precisely that humble faith of the simple people against the arrogance of the theologians and also against the detached, bourgeois, comfortable faith of the big cities.

We tried to maintain a simple, Catholic, faith. But our faith took on its coloration first in the country and then in the little city of Traunstein, where Catholicism was really deeply interwoven with the living culture of that land and its history. It was, I would say, inculturation. It was thus an expression [of faith] that suited us and that our own history had brought us.

We were very patriotic Bavarians already by family tradition. Our father came from lower Bavaria, and you know that in the Bavarian politics of the nineteenth century there were two currents. There was one more oriented to the *Reich* and more German-nationalistic. The other was a more Bavarian-Austrian, also Francophile-Catholic leaning. My family belonged very clearly to this second current, which was very consciously and patriotically Bavarian and proud of our history. My mother came from Tyrol, but there too, you know, this southern German-Catholic element was very strong and had a living presence in another way. In this respect we identified very much with our own history and were also aware that it was a respectable history. This history had nothing to do with nationalistic history, which then led to the great calamities of 1933 to 1945. On the contrary, the very catastrophe of nationalism confirmed us in our own conception of history.

Were there father–son conflicts?

In some sense there certainly always were. However, I had a very close relationship with my father. This was really due to the fact that already in his last year of work he took rather long sick leaves. The Third Reich went terribly against his grain, and he tried to get out of service as early as possible. In these months he took a lot of hikes with me. At that point we became very close to each other. When later all three children were studying and my family's financial situation had become very difficult after my father's retirement, so that my mother went back to doing seasonal work as a cook in Reit im Winkl, I was alone at home with my father. He told a lot of stories; he had a great gift for storytelling. So as we walked and told stories, we grew very close. Moreover, his religion and his decided antagonism toward the regime were convincing to us. His simple power to convince came out of his inner honesty. So his attitude became a model for us, even though it stood against what had public currency at the time.

So how did he express himself toward the regime?

He was in the civil service until 1937. In Tittmoning we lived through the so-called "time of struggle", the final period of the Weimar Republic. I was still very small, but I can remember how he suffered. He had subscribed to *Der gerade Weg*, an anti-Nazi newspaper; I can still remember the caricatures of Hitler. He was very sharp in his terminology. The approaching seizure of power, which he saw coming, was also the chief reason why we went to the village. There the situation was obviously much less tense, even though there were unfortunately a large number of Nazis among the country farmers. He made no public opposition; that wouldn't have been possible even in the village. But at home, whenever he read the newspaper, he almost had fits of rage. He always expressed his indignation vigorously and always spoke freely to people whom he could trust. Above all, he never joined any organization, even though he was a civil servant.

Were you in the Hitler Youth?

At first we weren't, but when the compulsory Hitler Youth was introduced in 1941, my brother was obliged to join. I was still too young, but later, as a seminarian, I was registered in the HY. As soon as I was out of the seminary, I never went back. And that was difficult, because the tuition reduction, which I really needed, was tied to proof of attendance at the HY. Thank goodness, there was a very understanding mathematics teacher. He himself was a Nazi but an honest man, who said to me, "Just go once and get the document so that we have it . . ." When he saw that I simply didn't want to, he said, "I understand, I'll take care of it", and so I was able to stay free of it.

What would you have wanted to be when you were still a child? Were there models?

I couldn't really say that I had clear models. As is the case with children, ideas often change radically. At some point a house painter who painted a wall impressed me so much that I wanted to emulate him. When later Cardinal Faulhaber paid a visit to our region, with his imposing purple, he impressed me all the more, so that I said, I would like to become something like that.

House painter and cardinal—quite different professions.

Yes, you're right, but there you see that a child doesn't reflect on these things; he bases himself on the optical effect. Pretty early on, already in elementary school, a desire to teach awoke in me. I'm grateful that this desire fit so well with the idea of the priesthood. But I would say that teaching, the transmission of what you've discovered, was early on something that excited me. Writing too. Already in elementary school I began to write. To write poems and so forth.

What sort of poems?

Whatever came to mind; about things of everyday life, Christmas poems, nature poetry. It was simply a sign of the fact that I took delight in expressing myself and above all in passing it on as well. So whenever I learned something, I also wanted to pass it on.

Didn't you ever want to have a family of your own, and weren't you ever in love with a woman? We know about Pope John Paul II that he was very much in love during his youth.

Well, I would say that my plans never progressed as far as a clear desire for a family. But of course I, too, was touched by friendship.

How did your vocation happen? When did you know what your destiny was? You said once that "I was convinced, I myself don't know how, that God wanted something from me, and it could be attained only by my becoming a priest."

At any rate, there was no lightning-like moment of illumination when I realized I was meant to become a priest. On the contrary, there was a long process of maturation, and the decision had to be thought through and constantly rewon. I couldn't date the decision, either. But the feeling that God had a plan for each person, for me too, became clear for me early on. Gradually it became clear to me that what he had in mind had to do with the priesthood.

Did you have something like flashes of illumination—or something like illumination—at a later time?

Well, I haven't had illuminations in the classical sense, if by that you mean something half-mystical. I am a perfectly ordinary Christian. But in a broader sense faith certainly gives one light. As one reflects on that faith, one certainly seems, to say it with Heidegger, to get a glimpse of the clearing from the various paths through the woods.

You once wrote that "all that is, is a stream of thought. The creative spirit is the origin and the sustaining ground of all things. All that is, is by its origin intelligible, because it comes from creative reason."

These sentences are really an attempt to state what the Christian doctrine of creation has developed and implies in terms of philosophy. That nothing is simply there, but what is there is there on the basis of a creative energy, and that is in turn not some dead energy but is reason and love—and in that respect everything created is ultimately intelligible. That is, I believe, the Christian philosophy of creation. And when it is believed and pondered, it gives one light, but one cannot speak in this case of "illumination" in the common sense.

After you decided to become a priest—didn't certain self-doubts emerge at some time, temptations or seductions?

They did, to be sure. In the six years of theological study one encounters so many human problems and questions. Is celibacy right for me? Is being a parish priest right for me? Those were indeed questions not always easy to deal with. I always had the basic direction before me, but there was no lack of crises.

What crises emerged? Can you give an example?

In the years when I was studying theology in Munich I had to struggle above all with two questions. I was fascinated by academic theology. I found it wonderful to enter into the great world of the history of faith; broad horizons of thought and faith opened up before me, and I was learning to ponder the primordial questions of human existence, the questions of my own life. But it became clearer and clearer that there is more to the priestly vocation than enjoying theology, indeed, that work in the parish can often lead very far away from that and makes completely different demands. In other words, I couldn't study theology in order to become a professor, although this was my secret wish. But the Yes to the priesthood meant that I had to say Yes to the whole task, even in its simplest forms.

Since I was rather diffident and downright unpractical, since I had no talent for sports or administration or organization, I had to ask myself whether I would be able to relate to people—whether, for example, as a chaplain I would be able to lead and inspire Catholic youth, whether I would be capable of giving religious instruction to the little ones, whether I could get along with the old and sick, and so forth. I had to ask myself whether I would be ready to do that my whole life long and whether it was really my vocation.

Bound up with this was naturally the question of whether I would be able to remain celibate, unmarried, my whole life long. Since the university had been destroyed and there was as yet no place for theology students, we lived for two years in the Fürstenried Castle with its buildings on the edge of the city. There not only professors and students but also male and female students lived at such close quarters that the daily encounter definitely made the question of renunciation and its inner meaning a practical one. I often pondered these questions as I walked in the beautiful park of Fürstenried and naturally in the chapel, until finally at my diaconal ordination in the fall of 1950 I was able to pronounce a convinced Yes.

Did you have to join the army at the end of the war?

Yes. From 1943 on, the seminarians in Traunstein were all conscripted into antiaircraft work at Munich. I was sixteen years old, and for a whole year, from August '43 to September '44, we did our service. In Munich we were attached to the Max *Gymnasium*, so we also got lessons on the side. The subjects were reduced, but still we got a useful amount of instruction. On the one hand, this was naturally not pleasant, but, on the other hand, the camaraderie of the time also had its excitement.

So what did you do in antiaircraft?

A battery was divided into two main elements, the artillery

and the range-finding section. I was in the range-finding section. We already had the first electronic and optical instruments to locate the approaching aircraft and to give the readings to the artillery. Besides the regular drills we had to be at the instrument at every alarm. What then became increasingly unpleasant was that there were more and more night alarms, and many nights were pretty much ruined.

Did you experience the bombing in Munich?

Yes. At that time I was in a third division, communications, which operated the whole telephone system. We had an important position in Gilching near Ammer Lake, because the Americans attacked Munich from the south, from the lakes. In addition, the Oberpfaffenhofen airplane factory, where the first jet fighters were built, was in the neighborhood. So we saw the first German jets take off. There was a series of attacks there; we really experienced the war firsthand.

In the fall of '44 we were first discharged and passed to work duty. I was stationed for two months on the Austrian-Hungarian border, just when Hungary had capitulated to the Russians. At that time we threw up huge embankments, tank traps, and the like. I finally came to the infantry. However, I had the great good fortune to be called to Traunstein. When we were deployed, there was a very good officer who was obviously anti-Nazi and who tried to find ways to help each of his men. He sent me home to Traunstein, so that my infantry service was relatively harmless. I was also taken prisoner there and afterward ended up in an American prisoner-of-war camp in Ulm with about forty to fifty thousand prisoners. I was released on June 19, 1945.

What are your memories of the end of the war?

At that time we were in the airport in Aibling. During the entire six weeks of my imprisonment, we slept out of doors on the ground, which wasn't always pleasant. The Americans couldn't supply huts or quarters for those enormous masses of prisoners. We had no calendar, nothing, so we had to make an effort to figure out the date. There was also no news. Then the only thing we noticed was that on May 8 the Americans, who were always firing a few shots in the air, suddenly started shooting like mad—it was a real fireworks show. Then the rumor spread that the war was over, that Germany had surrendered. At that point we breathed a sigh of relief, of course, because we thought that our release must be approaching as well and that nothing else could happen to us. However, the rumor immediately spread that we shouldn't rejoice too soon because the Americans would now start fighting against the Russians. We would be armed again and sent against the Russians. However, I couldn't imagine that the Alliance had come to pieces so quickly and didn't believe that report. I was simply happy that the war was over and only hoped this business wouldn't last too long.

The Young Professor

You once said, "When I began to study theology I also started getting interested in intellectual problems. This was because they unveiled the drama of my life and above all the mystery of truth." What did you mean by that?

I would say that that's a bit "pompously" expressed. All it means is that when you are studying theology, your intention is not to learn a trade but to understand the faith, and this presupposes, as we said a while ago, using the words of Augustine, that the faith is true, that, in other words, it opens the door to a correct understanding of your own life, of the world, and of men. This study also automatically throws you into the whole intellectual debate of Western history. From the very beginning, the faith is interwoven, on the one hand, with the Jewish heritage and, on the other, with the Latin and Greek heritage. And this obviously applies to its modern history. In that sense, the study of theology was tied to the question: What is really true, what can we know?

In our seminary in Freising there was a very vibrant atmosphere in those days. People had come back from the war, some from six-year-long participation in the war, and they were now filled with a real intellectual and literary hunger. With questions, too, of course, questions posed by what they had just lived through. People were reading Gertrud von le Fort, Ernst Wiechert and Dostoevski, Elisabeth Langgässer, everything that was around in the way of literature at the time. Those who studied in Munich had made the acquaintance of Heidegger and Jaspers via Steinbüchel, who taught moral theology at the time. There was a great intellectual élan, and one got swept up with it.

Which intellectual current interested and fascinated you in particular?

Heidegger and Jaspers interested me a great deal, along with personalism as a whole. Steinbüchel wrote a book entitled *The Revolution of Thought* [*Der Umbruch des Denkens*], in which he recounted with great verve the revolutionary shift from the dominance of neo-Kantianism to the personalistic phase. That was a key book for me. But then from the beginning Saint Augustine interested me very much—precisely also insofar as he was, so to speak, a counterweight to Thomas Aquinas.

He says: "Reprimand troublemakers, comfort the fainthearted, refute opponents." That's how he defines his office.

He was a real bishop. He wrote huge tomes, too, so that one wonders how he managed to accomplish that next to all the odds and ends he had to do. But as a bishop he had above all to deal constantly with all the quarrels of the state and with the needs of the little people, and he tried to keep this structure together. It was an unsettled time, the barbarian invasions were beginning. In that sense, he was a man who was by no means floating in the clouds.

In the organization of the empire at that time, the bishop was also a sort of justice of the peace. He held a certain level of jurisdiction and had to decide routine civil litigations. So he lived amid all that day by day and in doing so tried to mediate to men the peace of Christ, the gospel. In this sense, he is also an exemplar, because although he had such a great yearning for meditation, for intellectual work, he gave himself up to the small details of everyday life and wanted to be there for people.

What moved me then, however, was not so much his office as shepherd, which I was not familiar with in that way, but the freshness and vitality of his thought. Scholasticism has its greatness, but everything is very impersonal. You need some time to enter in and recognize the inner tension. With Augustine, however, the passionate, suffering, questioning man is always right there, and you can identify with him.

You finally became interested in Bonaventure's theology of history. How did that happen?

It was actually by chance. Since my dissertation had dealt with the ancient Church, my teacher, Professor Söhngen, remarked that my postdoctoral work should treat the Middle Ages or the modern period. In any case, I was supposed to do research of some kind on Bonaventure's concept of revelation. Söhngen knew that the Augustinian school appealed to me more than the Thomistic, so he set me to work on Bonaventure, whom he himself knew quite well and venerated.

Fundamental theology has to do with "revelation". What is revelation, actually? Can there be such a thing? And questions like that. After I started and worked through the texts, I discovered that for Bonaventure revelation was inseparable from the Franciscan adventure, and that in turn this adventure was connected with Joachim of Fiore, who foresaw a third age, the Age of the Holy Spirit, as a new period of revelation. Joachim had also calculated the time when this was to begin. And this chronology coincides, strangely enough, with the life of Saint Francis, who really did introduce a quite new phase in the history of the Church. So the Franciscans, at least a significant current of them, soon had the feeling that Joachim had predicted what they in fact were. Here was the new Age of the Holy Spirit; here is the simple, new, poor people of God that doesn't need any worldly structures.

The result was that the concept of revelation wasn't simply put somewhere at the beginning, in some far-off place, but revelation was now bound up with history. It was a process that progressed in history and had now entered into a new phase. So for Bonaventure revelation was no longer an abstract subject but was bound up with the interpretation of his own Franciscan history.

What did that open up for you?

There are two main issues. One could be expressed as follows. If the Christian faith is tied to a revelation that was concluded long ago, isn't it condemned to look backward and to chain man to a past time? Can it then keep pace with the continuing march of history? Does it still have anything at all to say to history? Mustn't it gradually grow old and end up being simply unrealistic? Bonaventure's answer to these questions was to underscore forcefully the connection between Christ and the Holy Spirit according to the Gospel of John. The word revealed in history is definitive, but it is inexhaustible, and it unceasingly discloses new depths. In this sense, the Holy Spirit, as the interpreter of Christ, speaks with his word to every age and shows it that this word always has something new to say. Unlike Joachim of Fiore, Bonaventure doesn't project the Holy Spirit into a future period, but it's always the age of the Holy Spirit. The age of Christ is the age of the Holy Spirit.

This brings up the second question on the agenda, the question of eschatology and utopia. It's hard for man to hope only for the beyond, or for a new world after the destruction of the present one. He wants a promise in history. Joachim concretely formulated such a promise and so prepared the way for Hegel, as Father de Lubac showed. Hegel, in turn, furnished the intellectual model for Marx. Bonaventure objected to the kind of utopia that deceives man. He also opposed an enthusiastic, spiritual-anarchical concept of the Franciscan movement and prevailed with a sober and realistic concept, something that offended many, and still does. But he saw the answer to the question of utopia precisely in such non-utopian communities that were nonetheless driven by the passion of faith. They don't work for a world beyond tomorrow; they work instead so that there may be something of the light of paradise present in this world today. They live in "utopian" fashion, as far as possible, by renouncing possessions, self-determination, and eros and its fulfillment. So a breath of fresh air comes into the world, breaking through its constraints and bringing God very close, right into the midst of this world.

After your studies you first spent a year in pastoral work. I have been told that your main task was to conduct funerals.

No, that's not correct. When I was an assistant pastor I had to teach sixteen hours of religious education a week. Not only that, but I had to do that in six different grades, from the second to the eighth. That's a hefty bundle of work, especially when you're just beginning. In terms of the amount of time, that was my main occupation, which I came to love, because I very quickly formed a good relationship with the children. For me it was interesting to step outside the intellectual sphere for a change and to learn to talk with children. It was quite a wonderful thing to translate the whole world of abstract concepts in such a way that it also said something to a child.

Every Sunday I had three homilies, one children's homily and two for adults. To my amazement, the children's Mass was the best attended of all, because now suddenly the adults started coming too. I was the only curate, and in addition to that I also took care of the whole youth ministry alone every evening. Every week I had baptisms and also a lot of burials, that's correct, where I rode right through Munich on my bicycle.

Were you completely alone?

Yes, but I had a very good pastor, Monsignor Blumschein. Now, he was really the model of a good pastor; not an intellectual, but a man who was completely committed to his task and who was also very kind.

You were one of the youngest professors in Germany, and the students sat up and took notice. An early student recounts that you put things in a new light and brought a new approach to them.

I believe that being young also had something to do with that. And naturally for my courses I didn't just cobble something together from the textbooks, but I tried, in the style of Saint Augustine, to place as much of the material as possible in a clear relationship to the present and to our own struggles. I suppose that that made the students sit up and listen.

In an early encomium, Professor Wolfgang Beinert had this to say about the theologian Joseph Ratzinger: Your theology was sovereign and masterly and inseparable from your person. "He has an alert analytical intelligence, coupled with a vigorous power of synthesis." You could immediately uncover and get to the core of theological weaknesses. Your language had a "classical radiance". Do you recognize yourself in this description?

I think that's a bit too high-flown, as is usual with encomia. Naturally, I strove to make clean analyses, and for that very reason I also tried to help my doctoral students to see through the weak points of an argument. For me a very important experience, also humanly speaking, was the fact that I didn't work with the doctoral candidates individually; rather, every week we worked together for about two hours, and each one took turns presenting the results of his research and submitting them to discussion. I think that everyone gained by that.

Very soon we expanded that by visiting great men as well. We were once with Congar in Strasbourg; another time we visited Karl Barth in Basel, whereas we invited Karl Rahner to visit us. That was a very lively circle indeed. We didn't spare one another anything either. We knew that there wasn't any animosity among us, but that we were helping each other by analyzing things critically. On the other hand, we also tried not to get stuck in analysis but to go on to synthesis.

What would you yourself see as specific about your theology or the way you do theology?

I began with the theme of the Church, and it is present in everything. Only, in dealing with the Church it was important to me, and it has become increasingly important, that the Church not be an end in herself but exist so that God may be seen. In that respect I would say that I study the theme of the Church with the intention of opening a vista onto God. And in this sense God is the real central theme of my endeavors.

I have never tried to create a system of my own, an individual theology. What is specific, if you want to call it that, is that I simply want to think in communion with the faith of the Church, and that means above all to think in communion with the great thinkers of the faith. The aim is not an isolated theology that I draw out of myself but one that opens as widely as possible into the common intellectual pathway of the faith. For this reason exegesis was always very important. I couldn't imagine a purely philosophical theology. The point of departure is first of all the word. That we believe the word of God, that we try really to get to know and understand it, and then, as I said, to think it together with the great masters of the faith. This gives my theology a somewhat biblical character and also bears the stamp of the Fathers, especially Augustine. But it goes without saying that I try not to stop with the ancient Church but to hold fast to the great high points of thought and at the same time to bring contemporary thought into the discussion.

Truth is the central concept in your thought. "Co-workers of the Truth" was later also your episcopal motto. Shouldn't one also be a co-worker of reality, or a co-worker of wisdom?

One is impossible without the other, for truth and reality belong together. A truth without reality would be a pure abstraction. And a truth that isn't concretized in "human wisdom" wouldn't, for its part, be a truth that man had really received, but a caricature of truth.

In the beginning, this theme wasn't so central for me. In the course of my intellectual life I experienced very acutely the problem of whether it isn't actually presumptuous to say that we can know the truth—in the face of all our limitations. I also asked myself to what extent it might not be better to suppress this category. In pursuing this question, however, I was able to observe and also to grasp that relinquishing truth doesn't solve anything but, on the contrary, leads to the tyranny of caprice. In that case, the only thing that can remain is really what we decide on and can replace at will. Man is degraded if he can't know truth, if everything, in the final analysis, is just the product of an individual or collective decision.

In this way it became clear to me how important it is that we don't lose the concept of truth, in spite of the menaces and perils that it doubtless carries with it. It has to remain as a central category. As a demand on us that doesn't give us rights but requires, on the contrary, our humility and our obedience and can lead us to the common path. Out of a rather long struggle with the intellectual situation in which we find ourselves, the primacy of the truth became evident to me, a primacy that, as I said, can't be grasped in a purely abstract way but naturally demands integration into wisdom.

Your brother gives us the following characterization of you: "He is not aggressive at all, but when it's necessary to fight, he does his part, as a matter of conscience." Are you a man of conscience?

I try to be. I'm not bold enough to claim that I am. But it does seem to me very important not to put seeking approval or accommodating the feelings of the group above the truth. That's always a big temptation. The appeal to conscience can, of course, shift into obstinacy, in which you think you always have to be against everything. But, understood in the proper sense, a man who listens to his conscience and for whom the truth that he has recognized, the good, is above approval and acceptance, is really an ideal and a model for me. And personalities such as Thomas More, Cardinal Newman, and other great witnesses—we have the great men who were persecuted by the Nazi regime, Dietrich Bonhoeffer, for example—are great examples for me.

However, as you once remarked, such a man has to stress "the primacy of truth over goodness". A point of view that's not without its risks, I think. Wouldn't that correspond to the image of the Grand Inquisitor as Dostoevski portrayed him?

As for that citation, you have to read the whole context, of course. Goodness is understood there in the sense of a false good-naturedness, "I don't want any trouble." That is a very frequent attitude that can be observed even in the political sphere, where politicians don't want to spoil things. People would sooner put up with false, impure, untruthful, and evil things than cause or have problems. There is a willingness to purchase well-being, success, public regard, and approval from the reigning opinion by dispensing with the truth. It wasn't my intention to object to goodness in general. Truth can be successful and victorious, if at all, only with goodness. What I meant was a caricature of goodness that is rather widespread. The fact is that under the pretext of goodness people neglect conscience. They place acceptance, the avoidance of problems, the comfortable pursuit of their existence, the good opinion of others, and good-naturedness above truth in the scale of values.

People attribute to you an "old Bavarian persistence" as well as a "sincere and simple piety". All of this, they say, flows from a depth that can only be described as baroque. Thanks to an exact knowledge of the abysses of human existence, you have "kept intact a sense of the joyful beauty of the redeemed creation". But isn't that a contradiction?

Let's put it like this. Life doesn't exist in contradictions, but it does exist in paradoxes. A joyfulness based on willful blindness to the horrors of history would ultimately be a lie or a fiction, a kind of withdrawal. But the converse is also true. Those who have lost the capacity to see that even in an evil world the Creator still shines through are at bottom no longer capable of existing. They become cynical, or they have to say farewell to life altogether. In this sense, the two things belong together: the refusal to evade the abysses of history and of man's existence, and then the insight that faith gives us that the good is present, even if we aren't always able to connect the two things. Particularly when one has to resist evil it's all the more important not to fall into a gloomy moralism that doesn't allow itself any joy but really to see how much beauty there is, too, and to draw from it the strength needed to resist what destroys joy.

Is it possible to play at theology like a game, in the way that Hermann Hesse described it in his The Glass Bead Game?

That would be too little. I mean, there is certainly an element of playfulness. But ultimately, it's not, as Hesse thinks in *The Glass Bead Game*, a question of a constructed world, a sort of mathematics of thinking, but of confronting reality. And by that I mean the whole compass and the whole claim of reality. To that extent, the element of play is included, because it is, after all, an authentic element of our existence, a component, but it wouldn't be enough to characterize the right way of doing theology.

Another of Hesse's works, Steppenwolf, *is among your favorite books. The novel is considered one of the most significant documents of cultural pessimism and early existentialism. On rereading it, one finds the record of a neurotically hypersensitive person, whose agonizing self-analysis is at the same time the attempt to diagnose the illness of the time. Does this description also have something to do with you?*

No. For me the book was a real discovery because of its diagnostic and prognostic power. It anticipated, in a certain way, the problems that we subsequently lived through in the sixties and seventies. The novel, as you know, is actually about one person, but one who analyzes himself into so many personalities that the analysis finally leads to self-disintegration. Stretching the self too far here also means destroying it. In other words, there aren't just two souls in one breast; man disintegrates altogether. I didn't read this to identify with it but as a key that with visionary power pierces through and exposes the problem of modernity's isolated and self-isolating man.

The idea of a multi-optional personality, the idea that modern man no longer has a clear-cut identity, that today he's one thing and tomorrow something else, is a vision that only in our own time is really blossoming. Anything is possible. The individual is no longer tied to a certain pattern; life is accordingly an infinite game played with every conceivable variation.

But in that very arbitrariness it also becomes empty. Life, in which we are confronted with death and suffering, is too serious to be a mere game. Man can lose his identity, but he cannot get rid of his responsibility, and because of that responsibility his past always catches up with him again.

You are a professor now; you've taught in Bonn, Münster, Tübingen, and Regensburg. You started in a reformist direction. Finally, the German Cardinal Joseph Frings of Cologne makes you his advisor. And now something astonishing occurs. The Council has been long prepared and planned down to the last detail—until you write a sensational speech for Cardinal Frings. And suddenly everything is again in disarray, and the assembly whose documents have already been worked out has to make a fresh start. What exactly happened?

You should never, as Karl Rahner often said, overestimate the role of an individual. Now, the Council was a very large body, and while individuals certainly generated decisive impulses, the reason they could do so was that others desired the same thing. Perhaps others couldn't formulate it, but the willingness was there; people were on the lookout for something.

The Council Fathers did not come together with the intention simply of adopting ready-made texts and, so to speak, rubber-stamping them but, in accord with their office, of struggling to find the word that had to be said in that hour. There was the idea that we had to take the task in hand ourselves, not in order to turn the faith upside down, but, on the contrary, to serve it properly. In this sense, Frings' introductory speech (which had points in common with that of Cardinal Liénart of Lille) actually put into words the common awareness already present among the Fathers.

So what did you write in this speech?

The very first one was not written by me, nor was it a speech in the strict sense. The situation was that proposals had already been worked out in Rome for the composition of the Curia, the commissions. And the expectation was that there would be an immediate vote on the basis of those proposed lists. Now, many of the Fathers didn't want that. Then both Cardinal Liénart and Cardinal Frings rose to their feet and said that we cannot simply vote at this time, that we have to get in contact with one another in order to find out who is suitable for what, that the elections have to be postponed. That was the first drumbeat at the beginning of the Council. When you reflect, it wasn't all that rabid, either. It was normal for them to try themselves to find suitable candidates. That was an impulse that came spontaneously to both of them and that also corresponded to the desires of the assembly.

The second thing—I may be compressing several events together in this account—was that, concretely, when the text on revelation was to be proposed for discussion, Cardinal Frings—and there, admittedly, I did play a part—explained that the text as it was then worded was not an adequate starting point. It was, he said, necessary to start from the ground up, to rework the document within the Council itself. That really sounded the alarm. It was what really first led to the saying that we will rework the texts ourselves.

In the third speech, which has become famous, the subject was the necessity of reforming the methods of the Holy Office and the need for a transparent procedure there. Those are the speeches that stuck in the mind of the public.

Had this sounding of the alarm been planned? The effect of the speech could not have surprised you?

It may have surprised some people, but it also corresponded to an expectation. Cardinal Frings had prior contacts with individuals that indicated this kind of expectation. It was in keeping with, so to speak, the inner logic of the assembly to say something like that.

You were considered a progressive theologian. As a professor you were
at this time a star yourself, your lectures were filled to overflowing. You
debated openly about frankness, tolerance. You also thundered against
the neoscholastic rigidity of Rome and severely reproached the Vatican
authorities for leading the Church into rigidity. As a young theolo-
gian you complained at the time that the Church had "reins that are
too tight, too many laws, many of which have helped to leave the
century of unbelief in the lurch, instead of helping it to redemption".
One can probably say that without your involvement the reforms of
the Second Vatican Council would have been unthinkable.

I feel that you are quite overestimating my role. If there had
not also been a large group of like-minded people, no individual, not to mention a theologian who was totally unknown around the world, could have had any importance.
Not even if he spoke through the mouth of an important,
well-known cardinal.

After Pope John had convoked the Council and had given
it its motto of *"aggiornamento"*, taking a leap forward and up-
dating the faith, there was a very strong desire among the
Council Fathers really to venture something new and to leave
behind the habitual scholastic framework, also to risk a new
freedom. That went from South America to Australia.
Whether there was already a similar desire in Africa, I cannot
say. In any case, there was such a desire present in wide seg-
ments of the episcopate.

I cannot recall the individual sentences you cited, but it is
correct that I was of the opinion that scholastic theology, in
the form it had come to have, was no longer an instrument
for bringing faith into the contemporary discussion. It had to
get out of its armor; it also had to face the situation of the
present in a new language, in a new openness. So a greater
freedom also had to arise in the Church. Of course, the

pathos of a young man also played a part in this. But on the whole it was an awareness that could be noticed all across the Church, an awareness that was connected with the feeling of emergence in the postwar period—and with the hope that now, at last, a new hour of Christianity was also possible.

You yourself, as you have stressed again and again, have always tried to remain faithful to Vatican II, "without nostalgia for a yesterday that is irrevocably past". On the other hand, not many years after the ending of the Council you also spoke of an "anti-spirit" of the Council and made a negative assessment. A leap forward had been expected, but now we were reaping a "process of decline". What had gone awry?

That is the great question we all ask ourselves. The fact that the expectations weren't met can be documented in purely empirical, statistical terms. And today, in fact, it is above all progressive people who speak of a "winter of the Church". That we didn't experience a new hour of the Church, that much fell apart—to be sure, alongside new breakthroughs— no one can contest.

Why did it turn out this way? I would tentatively say two things. First, we had doubtless expected too much. The Church is something we can't make ourselves. We can do our part, but the weal and the woe do not depend on our activity alone. The great currents of history have, in fact, gone their way. In part, they simply had not been rightly assessed. That is the first thing: there was an overexpectation that was perhaps not quite right in the sense that we wanted to see Christianity grow in breadth and did not recognize that the hour of the Church can also look quite different.

The second thing is that there was quite a significant differ- ence between what the Fathers wanted and what was conveyed to the public and then became fixed in the general consciousness. The Fathers wanted to update the faith—but this was precisely in order to present it with its full impact. Instead, the impression increasingly gained hold that reform consisted in simply jettisoning ballast, in making it easier for ourselves. Reform thus seemed really to consist, not in a radicalization of the faith, but in any kind of dilution of the faith.

However, we increasingly see that choosing the right form of simplifying, concentrating on, and deepening the essentials is not simply a matter of lightening loads, adapting, and making concessions. In other words, there are basically two concepts of reform. The first concept has more to do with renouncing external power and external factors, in order to live all the more by faith. The other consists in making history more comfortable, to caricature this approach somewhat. And then things go awry, of course.

This false interpretation has obviously persisted until today. For curiously everyone appeals to the spirit of the Council, both those groups who see themselves as reformers as well as those who count themselves among the preservers. The heritage of the Council, you had already prophesied in 1975, "has not yet been revealed. It still awaits its hour, and this will come; I am certain about that."

Yes, it is correct that there are two interpretations of the Council. However, it is becoming ever clearer that the texts of the Council are wholly in continuity with the faith. For this reason, there are now many people who are already saying that the texts are only initial approaches. It is necessary to discern certain directions in the texts but then to detach oneself from them. However, with this approach we are no longer speaking of the Council. Of course, we must not make the texts into dead letters, but their authentic message, which can be recognized through objective interpretation, is the great heritage of the Council. Precisely from that point we must take it up, interpret it, understand it. And precisely in this way it does unleash an enormous variety of new impulses, even with respect to the Church's new relation to the world, with the declaration on religious freedom, and so forth.

It goes without saying, above all, that there are ways of deepening and encouraging the faith that are yet to be exploited. What I would like to stress in any case is this: The true inheritance of the Council lies in its texts. When one interprets them soundly and thoroughly, then one is preserved from extremisms in both directions; and then there really is a path that still has a long future ahead.

Did your assessment of the abuse of the Council also have something to do with the student revolt in Europe? Apparently there was an abrupt change during your time in Tübingen. The previously celebrated professor of theology, who was considered progressive, was suddenly an object of hostility. Students snatched the microphone from him. The events must obviously have been a shock for you. Later you said: "In these years I learned when a discussion had to stop because it was changing into a lie and when resistance was necessary in order to preserve freedom."

The microphone was never snatched from me. Nor did I ever have problems with the students, but rather with the group that could be classed with the so-called non-professorial staff. My courses in Tübingen were always very well received; contact with the students was very good. But it is true I saw a new spirit creeping in, a spirit in which fanatical ideologies made use of the spirit of Christianity, and it was there that the lie really became evident to me. Here I saw very clearly and also really experienced that there were incompatible concepts of reform. That there was an abuse of the Church and the faith, which were enlisted as instruments of power, but for totally different purposes and with totally different thoughts and ideas. The unanimous will to serve the faith had come to pieces. Instead of that there was an instrumentalization by ideologies that were tyrannical, brutal, and cruel. That experience made it clear to me that the abuse of the faith had to be resisted precisely if one wanted to uphold the will of the Council. As I said, I myself had no problems with the students. But I did see how real tyranny was exercised, even in brutal forms.

To give a somewhat more concrete idea of the events of that time, I would like to cite here a reminiscence of those years recently published by my Protestant colleague Beyerhaus, with whom I collaborated closely. " 'So what is Jesus' Cross but the expression of a sado-masochistic glorification of pain?' And the 'New Testament is a document of inhumanity, a large-scale deception of the masses.' These two citations came, not from the polemics of Bolshevist atheist propaganda, but from a flyer disseminated among fellow students in the summer of 1969 by the union of Protestant theology students at the University of Tübingen. Its title was: 'Jesus the Lord—Partisan Käsemann'. In the spirit of the Marxist critique of religion, the flyer accused the Church of sharing in the guilt of capitalist exploitation of the poor, and it ascribed to traditional theology the function of propping up the system. The above-named New Testament scholar of Tübingen was said to take part in this. . . . I shall never forget one traumatic memory. My colleague Ulrich Wickert and I vainly made the request to a plenary assembly of the students that the union of Protestant theology students distance itself from the blasphemies expressed in that flyer. No—we were told—the flyer addressed serious socio-political effects that had to be confronted first for truth's sake. Professor Wickert's passionate appeal, 'The cry of "Cursed be Jesus!" must never again be heard in our midst!' went unheeded and unanswered" (P. Beyerhaus, "Der kirchlich-theologische Dienst des Albrecht-Bengel-Hauses", *Diakrisis* 17 [March 1969]: 9f.). It never got quite so bad in the union of Catholic theology students, but the basic current, which surged powerfully into it as well, was the same. So I knew what was at stake: anyone who wanted to remain a progressive in this context had to give up his integrity.

So it was not entirely a coincidence that your famous Introduction to Christianity *began with the story of "Lucky Jack"* [Hans im Glück].

Yes, that is correct. At that time, after I had seen the movement of the previous years, this story came to my mind, for here, too, Christianity was experienced primarily as a burden, just like the lump of gold in the fable. And it became more and more obvious to me that the way of reinterpretation, which was shaping up with increasing clarity, only exchanged it for something worse. The parable was actually perfectly suited to describe the situation at the time, even though this story had been written in 1967, and thus before the outbreak of these trends.

Many conjecture that this Hans is perhaps . . .

No, it has absolutely nothing to do with Hans Küng, I have to say that quite decidedly. An attack on him was the farthest thing from my mind.

You, too, could have become a great critic in the tradition of the Ger-
man rebels against the Church. What stopped you? Hans Küng sus-
pects that Paul VI urged some of the critical forces to prepare
themselves for leading positions.

I don't know anything about that. Paul VI had no such discussion with me, at any rate. I met him personally for the first
time in June of 1977, after my episcopal consecration. That I
was named archbishop of Munich in 1977 was a surprise, in
fact, a shock to me—in any case not a quid pro quo for op-
portunistic concessions. No. Although the constellations in
which I have found myself—and naturally also the periods of
life and their different influences—have led to changes and
development in the accents of my thought, my basic impulse,
precisely during the Council, was always to free up the authentic kernel of the faith from encrustations and to give this
kernel strength and dynamism. This impulse is the constant
of my life. It would also have ruled out my withdrawing into
an anti-Church opposition. Naturally the office gives an accentuation that isn't present as such when you are a professor.
But nonetheless what's important to me is that I have never
deviated from this constant, which from my childhood has
molded my life, and that I have remained true to it as the basic direction of my life.

You yourself have always made a point of subordinating your person-
ality to your task, and not vice versa. That obviously corresponds to
your concept of duty, obedience, and service, those concepts that in the
course of cultural upheavals have fallen into disrepute.

But there will surely be a return to them. For if there is no
willingness to subordinate oneself to a whole that one has
recognized and to let oneself be taken into its service, then

there can't be any common freedom. Man's freedom is always a shared freedom. It has to be borne together, and it therefore demands service. Naturally, these virtues, if we want to call them that, can also be abused, if one orders them to a false system. They can't, in fact, be good in themselves in a purely formal way but only in connection with the purpose to which they are ordered. This purpose is in my case the faith, God, Christ, and thus I have the certainty of conscience that it is rightly placed.

From a certain point on you waged a campaign against the theologians and also reacted with increasing severity to internal theological criticism. One of your main sayings is: "This is His Church and not a laboratory for theologians."

I wouldn't want to battle theologians, because then I would, after all, be fighting against myself. Theology is a very important and noble craft, and the theologian's activity is very important. Criticism and being critical is also part of that. What I did campaign against is a theology that loses its criteria and thus no longer performs its service rightly. Just what we were saying: We are servants and don't ourselves determine what the Church is. This is the decisive point for me. However, this expression, "it is his Church and not ours", is really a fork in the road for me: to acknowledge that we do not excogitate what the Church is but that we believe that *He* wants her and that we should try to recognize what *He* wants with her and place ourselves in this service.

Bishop and Cardinal

In 1977 Pope Paul VI appointed you, as a "leading theologian", to be the archbishop of Munich and Freising, and not long afterward you were named cardinal. Your task was: "Work in God's field." What were your concerns when you became the bishop of Munich?

I had, of course, very great doubts at first about whether I should or ought to accept the appointment. I had little pastoral experience. I felt that, in principle, I was called from the beginning to teach and believed that at this period of my life—I was fifty years old—I had found my own theological vision and could now create an *oeuvre* with which I would contribute something to the whole of theology. I also knew that my health was fragile and that this office would involve a great physical demand on me.

I then took counsel and was told that in an extraordinary situation such as we live in today, it is also necessary to accept things that don't seem to be in the direction of one's life from the beginning. Today, the problem of the Church is very closely tied to that of theology. In this situation, even theologians have to be available as bishops. So I accepted, with the intention, as I expressed it in my episcopal motto, of being *a* "co-worker of the truth". Co-worker was meant in the plural. In other words, in communion with other co-workers I would contribute my charism, if I may call it that, and contribute using the theological experience and competence that had been given to me, so that the Church might be rightly led in this hour and the heritage of the Council rightly appropriated.

The striking thing was above all your concern as a bishop for the moral physiognomy of the time. Your theme was the dissolution of tradition and authenticity. You denounced certain centrifugal forces that spun everything into confusion. Criticism of the times was probably nowhere expressed more radically and dramatically. You warned against the possessions and pleasures that dull the heart and spoke of the sneer of Mephistopheles appearing behind so many phenomena of the time. What drove you then? Did you have a presentiment of the future? Why did you devote yourself so passionately to the critique of society?

There is a lot of talk today about the Church's prophetic task. The word is sometimes misused. But it is true that the Church may never simply align herself with the *Zeitgeist*. The Church must address the vices and perils of the time; she must appeal to the consciences of the powerful and of the intellectuals, not to mention of those who want to live narrow-minded, comfortable lives while ignoring the needs of the time, and so forth. As a bishop I felt obliged to face this task. Moreover, the deficits were too obvious: exhaustion of the faith, decline in vocations, lowering of moral standards even among men of the Church, an increasing tendency toward violence, and much else. The words of the Bible and of the Church Fathers rang in my ears, those sharp condemnations of shepherds who are like mute dogs; in order to avoid conflicts, they let the poison spread. Peace is not the first civic duty, and a bishop whose only concern is not to have any problems and to gloss over as many conflicts as possible is an image I find repulsive.

Your tenure as the bishop of Munich was not without conflicts, yet you were respected as a "traditionalist" who "showed the soundest knowledge of the doctrinal tradition". As the Süddeutsche Zeitung *wrote at the time, "Of all the conservatives in the Church", you were "the one with the greatest capacity for dialogue". Now, your reputation quickly changed, at least from the time when you were named Prefect of the Congregation for the Doctrine of the Faith in 1981. "Not all news that comes from Rome will be pleasant", as you already anticipated in your farewell remarks.*

Even today I am glad that in Munich I didn't dodge conflicts, because letting things drift is—as I have already said—the worst kind of administration I can imagine. From the very beginning it was clear to me that during my time in Rome I would have to carry out a lot of unpleasant tasks. But I think I may say that I have always sought dialogue and that it has also been very fruitful. We have now instituted forms of regular dialogue with the most important bishops' conferences and the superiors of major orders, and in so doing we have been able to resolve many problems that at first were like millstones blocking the way. Above all, very many good relationships with bishops from around the world have developed, relationships for which—I believe—both sides are thankful.

Did you feel that you were suited, perhaps even predestined, for this job?

That would be saying too much. Two or three years before, I, at least, would not have thought at all about something like this. The world of the Roman Curia was basically completely foreign to me; I had no connections with it. It wasn't until the Council that I got to see a bit of it, but rather from a distance and certainly not as something to which I was predestined.

Did you really know beforehand that the Pope from Poland, whom you in fact had already known for a long time before, would appoint you?

No. I met him in 1977 at the Synod. Our real acquaintance didn't originate until the conclave in 1978, so we hadn't known each other for very long. I spontaneously got along with him very well, but that he would think of me never crossed my mind.

Was that solely the decision of John Paul II?

I suppose so, but I have never asked him about it. It may also be that he asked for advice. I do think it was a very personal decision.

Was it rather an advantage or a disadvantage that you are a German?

We all know what Germans are supposed to be like. In that respect it's easy to attribute decisions that incur displeasure to German stubbornness. Fanatical attachment to principles, lack of flexibility, all of that is also seen as an expression of the German spirit. When the term *Panzerkardinal* was coined, it certainly involved this sort of allusion to the fact that I am German. On the other hand, no one has ever, at least to my face, treated my Germanness with hostility or overemphasized its importance. In fact, it has become known everywhere that I don't engage privately in politics but that I am part of a whole, so that what I do is not simply the expression of my private character as a German but comes out of the entire structure of curial ministries and offices.

What was it about the Pope from Poland that won your sympathy? Did you see an affinity of character?

The first thing that won my sympathy was his uncomplicated, human frankness and openness, as well as the cordiality that he radiated. There was his humor. You also sensed a piety that had nothing false, nothing external about it. You sensed that here was a man of God. Here was a person who had nothing artificial about him, who was really a man of God and, what is more, a completely original person who had a long intellectual and personal history behind him. You notice that about a person: he has suffered, he has also struggled on his way to this vocation. He lived through the whole drama of the German occupation, of the Russian occupation, and of the Communist regime. He blazed his own intellectual trail. He studied German philosophy intensively; he entered deeply into the whole intellectual history of Europe. And he also knew crucial points in the history of theology that lead far from the usual paths. This intellectual wealth, as well as his enjoyment of dialogue and exchange, these were all things that immediately made him likeable to me.

Both of you were considered highly cultured and sensitive, young and polemical. Both of you were, as one observer put it, basically "intelligent reformers and personalities of the Council, whose pessimism, however, made them regard today's world as poised on the brink of a universal catastrophe". Did you work out a detailed understanding about your common intentions and goals, about where you wanted to lead the Church?

No, not at all. The Pope told me that he intended to call me to Rome. I presented him with the reasons against it, and he said, let's consider all of this again. Then, after the assassination attempt, we spoke again, and he said that he still had the same intention. I replied that I felt so committed to theology that I wanted to retain the right to publish private works of my own and that I did not know whether that was compatible with my charge. But then it turned out that others before me had already done so. He then said, no, that is not an obstacle, we can do that. But there was never any sort of decision about a program.

The Congregation for the Doctrine of the Faith is not exactly one of the most popular institutions. No one can forget that it comes from the erstwhile Holy Inquisition. What did you want to stress in your new office?

First of all, I wanted to stress as vigorously as possible the collegial model rather than individual decision making and to underscore the role of the individual constituent elements. I also wanted to foster dialogue with theology and theologians, as well as with the bishops, for our immediate partners are actually the bishops. To what extent that has been successful, I don't dare to say. In any case, we have done a lot to strengthen contact with the bishops. We have traveled the continents, and everywhere we have gone we have spoken with the doctrinal commissions and the local bishops. Now we are beginning again by turns. We have multiplied encounters during the *ad limina* visits and have tried to expand the team of theological consultors and, especially, to keep the function of the Theological and Biblical Commissions as strong as possible. These were my priorities, and I am trying to promote them further.

Didn't it excite you to have influence?

Actually, I was, on the contrary, apprehensive in that regard, because if one wanted to advance one's own ideas, it would have been easy to put too much of one's own into the office. But to contribute my thinking, or to help and to make available what I can, in this difficult situation of the Church is something that motivates me.

Is there also a feeling of power in your job?

Yes, but to a very modest extent. For the power that we have is in reality very little. All we can do actually is appeal to the bishops, who in turn must appeal to the theologians or to the religious superiors. Or else we can attempt dialogue. There are, of course, also disciplinary measures, which we try to apply as sparingly as possible. After all, we don't have executive power. In any case, it always takes good will and a desire to serve the Church on the part of all.

I mean an awareness of power referred to your own person.

I have to say that perhaps, objectively speaking, there is a sort of power in general, but I, personally, don't feel particularly powerful. Ultimately, we have no weapons besides argument and appeal to our faith. The only thing that can give our work significance is that the Church backs it up and that the interested parties accept what we undertake. The feeling that I am someone powerful has hardly ever occurred to me.

During your homily before leaving for Rome, you put yourself in the position of a doubter who realized that what he had sown was coming to nothing and who wondered: "Is this job really necessary?" And further: "Don't we need a completely different Church and a totally different office? And he likewise felt desire born of a solitude grown more difficult, the question of whether celibacy, which wasn't the first thing desired but only accepted for the sake of another call, was meaningful. Everything had grown dark around him; he finally wanted to be a man like everyone else, just to be himself." It is tempting to make a connection between the doubter and the cardinal who tells this story.

Unfortunately, I can no longer recall this homily. Of course, even a believer has to face these questions. I've also explained in my *Introduction to Christianity* that faith never cuts off questions. That it could also become rigid if it no longer exposed itself to these questions. In this sense, these are not fictitious questions but questions that I had to ask myself. But they were, so to speak, given over to the basic confidence of the faith. Not that they were simply explained away by this faith. But they were in a certain sense cushioned by it.

The Prefect and His Pope

According to the Code of Canon Law, the task of your Congregation is to "promote . . . and protect sound doctrine, to correct errors, and to lead the erring back to the right path". I suppose that it isn't a comfortable role to have to look after everything, to admonish people constantly, to have to be strict with people. But there is also the idea that your Congregation is a completely inflexible and misanthropic association.

Anyone who really has to deal with us also sees that we're not inhuman but always try to find a reasonable solution. Ultimately, as in any society, the Church has to find the right balance between individual rights and the good of the community as a whole. The point here is that the good in virtue of which the Church exists and which keeps her together is the faith. On the one hand, those who, as it were, can't fight back intellectually have to be defended—against intellectual assault on what sustains their life. On the other hand, our work demands respect for the rights of the person concerned. And the juridical procedures that we have, and that we also try to keep improving, consist in correctly balancing these two things.

For the rest, we try to manage without sanctions and to find solutions through dialogue, so that the author explains himself better than he has so far. This means that we enter into contact with the respective bishop or religious superior, who in turn enters into dialogue with the interested party, so that the first move is not a punitive action but a reasonable step that leads to further development.

You have a staff of about forty collaborators. That is not many, considering that there are a billion Christians around the world. Where do you get your information? How do you know what is going on in the world?

The principal sources of information are the episcopal conferences and our meetings with the bishops. In addition to that, there are theological publications, which we try to follow via periodicals and books. We then inform the bishops' conferences about these. Each of the individual collaborators has his own sector, and here, too, he, in turn, relates the information that comes partly from theologians, partly from the large circle of collaborators, or, above all, from the bishops' conferences and the bishops.

Do you have to check everything personally; do you do all of this yourself? For example, does the Catechism *come from your pen?*

No, I simply couldn't have done that. I have to try to coordinate the work collegially and to direct it so that the process produces some results. In the case of the *Catechism*, we had many levels of collaboration. Our work group, properly speaking, was a commission of fifteen bishops from the various continents. This group created in turn a group of eight bishops who were the actual authors. These then charged an editor with coordinating the whole work. In that sense, you can say that we are common coauthors. Besides that, throughout the process we had "input", as they say today, that was very broad. In fact, we wrote to all the bishops and episcopal conferences personally, and we received a response from at least a thousand bishops.

Was there also "input" from the people of the Church themselves?

We assume that a bishop isn't presenting his private opinion but the faith of the Church, which also means the faith of his local Church and its way of believing. We can't take a survey of a billion Catholics. The bishop as such, after all, is also a representative, one who stands for a whole community. In that respect, there is no doubt that the word of the faithful reached us through the more than one thousand bishops.

Are there statements or formulations in the Catechism *that you personally think are not entirely apt?*

Yes. Not everything turned out equally well. That's clear.

Could you name a passage?

No. I can't say off the top of my head. We would have to go to the text. But I believe that the *Catechism* on the whole is a very thorough and good work, also a very readable one. We are constantly getting confirmations of this. A lot of people —not theologians, but simple people—tell us that they are really able to read and understand it. The reception in Germany continues to be modest at best, for many reasons. But in America, for example, which is also a very critical country, two million copies have been sold. In Asia it is just getting off the ground, but in South America and in Spain, as well as in France, the reception has been very good. In Great Britain, too. The wealth of patristic texts alone makes the *Catechism* a precious treasure-trove of citations. Of course, it's a book produced by human beings that can always be improved, but it is a good book.

And what do you find particularly successful about the book?

First of all, I believe that the introduction, which deals with faith, turned out very well. Large parts of the section on the Church and the sacraments turned out very well, and the whole theology of the liturgy—really good liturgists collaborated on that—is very beautiful and vibrant. And the part on prayer has a style very much its own. I think it turned out well.

How long did the work take to elaborate in its present form?

It took almost exactly five years. The 1985 synod had expressed the desire for the *Catechism*. The Pope then established the commission in 1986. We were able to start work around the fall of 1986. Then, after six years, we were able to present the *Catechism*.

About your work as Prefect: What guarantee do you have that the Congregation's decisions are really correct?

The first guarantee is that we don't simply invent anything ourselves but work within the great ideas of the faith. The second is that we consult widely when we make practical applications, and we don't adopt isolated opinions or make decisions until a convergence has emerged among a representative circle of consultors. What is important is that we don't go beyond what is already present in the faith—which naturally has to be applied—and that we then see that a reasonable consensus emerges.

Do you have a meditative way of preparing the work? It is said that you interiorize a lot of things, that you think things through yourself, assimilate them spiritually. You've also said that you have to meditate on this and that. What does that mean?

It's clear that you first have to inform yourself. The first step is always to familiarize yourself with the state of the question. Then you have to think things over in order to understand the logic of the whole, in order to assimilate it, to grasp it and also to put it in relation to the whole, as well as to take it into prayer. I think that the process goes from information to assimilation—and to dialogue, of course—and back to assimilation. Those are the steps.

How important in all this are inspirations, and, above all, how do you get them?

Well, you can't conjure them up, they have to come. But you also have to be cautious about them; they have to be verifiable in the logic of the whole. Besides, the presupposition for an "inspiration" is that you are not in a rush, that you also consider the idea in peace, and that you let it mature for a long time in yourself.

At the very beginning of your term of office, you had to deal with liberation theology and to reprimand theologians who doubted the infallibility of the Pope or criticized other dogmas. It is the way this was done that continues to shape your image, at least relative to Germany. Might you, in retrospect, have reacted too harshly? Even assuming you gave the right answers?

I would distinguish between my personal reactions and what we did officially. That in a personal controversy I occasionally react too harshly, I concede without further ado. But in what we did as a congregation, I think that we kept to the right measure. In dealing with liberation theology we also had to say something to help the bishops. In the end, there was the threat of a politicization of the faith that would have forced it into an irresponsible political partisanship, thus destroying the properly religious dimension. The widespread exodus to the sects is doubtless connected with such politicization. Today there is wide recognition that our instructions were necessary and went in the right direction. An outstanding example of the positive impulses that our instructions gave is the career of Gustavo Gutiérrez, who is regarded as the creator of liberation theology. We entered into dialogue with him—which I in part also carried on personally—and came to an ever greater agreement. That helped us to understand him, and he, on the other hand, saw the one-sidedness of his work and then really developed it further in the direction of a suitable form of liberation theology that really had a future.

Of course, there are also points of conflict that couldn't be settled. In the meantime, the geopolitical situation has totally changed the question of liberation theology. But when one looks back on these fifteen years, one must say that our interventions were on the mark and also proved to be a help, perhaps not at the first moment, but in the long run. Today, the episcopates that at the beginning were in part rather dubious now also take that for granted.

But there wasn't just dialogue; there was also the imposition of years of silence, of "penitential silence".

The phrase "penitential silence" was invented in Germany. We had simply said that for a year he shouldn't speak about this subject but should reflect on it and not travel around the world. Well, you can always discuss whether something like that is right or not, but, objectively considered, it wasn't bad to invite someone to reflect longer on a difficult question. Perhaps it would do us all some good were someone to tell us, you should stop talking about that for a while, you shouldn't keep publishing frenetically, but give things a chance to mature. I don't wish to continue the argument about how good the measure was. Boff, in any case, was supposed to have been able to continue teaching. However, he didn't do so that year. It was only this particular subject that he was not supposed to pursue further in lectures and books but was to let alone for a year. So this was similar, in fact, to what was done in the case of Küng, whom Paul VI had invited to stop publishing writings about infallibility and to rethink the subject.

Hans Küng obviously didn't want to avail himself of the invitation, nor did Boff. And it is legitimate to ask whether or not the measure helped the Church's image.

As the media conveyed it around the world, it certainly did not help at first. In the meantime, many have perhaps been given pause by historical developments and the path that Boff took, which, by the way, I don't presume to judge.

And about Hans Küng's path? I mean, he now hopes for a rehabilitation.

A little bit of demythologization is needed here. Hans Küng was deprived of the mandate to teach in the name and by the charge of the Church. That may have been bitter for him at first, but it was precisely what helped him to find his own totally personal path. For then he was free from obligatory lectures within the framework of the formation of theologians as well as from the examinations connected with that. He could then dedicate himself completely to his own topics. In a conversation in 1982 he himself confessed to me that he didn't want to go back to the previous position and that his present position was much better suited to him. He gradually moved away from the narrower questions of specialized theology and in this very way was able to find and develop his major themes. Now he has retired, and a new commission to teach in the name of the Church would be even more pointless than before. Nor is he interested in that at all. He would rather that his theology be recognized as a valid form of Catholic theology. But he has taken back nothing of his contestation of the papal office; indeed, he has further radicalized his positions. In Christology and in trinitarian theology he has further distanced himself from the faith of the Church. I respect his path, which he takes in accord with his conscience, but he should not then demand the Church's seal of approval but should admit that in essential questions he has come to different, very personal decisions of his own.

You have always insisted on seeing reality as it is and on not conforming to the modern Zeitgeist. Your analyses of the causes of the crises in the Church and the world have, in the meantime, been very often borne out. However, this has not done much for your image in public or in the media. Is this due to the certainty with which you defend your standpoint, to the severity of your language?

I am the last person who would know that. Nor do I know how many attentive readers I have and how many readers have a good memory. For when things turn out in a certain way, a lot of people do not remember that they actually confirm diagnoses that I had made. I tend to believe that it is due to the identification of my person with the office of the Prefect and to the concomitant aversion toward its whole function and toward the Magisterium as such. So a lot of people read everything I may say as part of a mechanism that basically wants to keep mankind in tutelage and not as a genuine, honest, intellectual attempt to understand the world and man.

Is it enough always to be right? I mean, right decisions often need the right moment and the right presentation. It's the tone that makes the music, they say.

Yes, and I am by all means open to criticism. We also try to do things better, as best we can, and to enter more and more into dialogue with the bishops and the religious superiors in order to find the right way. But that doesn't rule out in principle, of course, that you may have to resort to a resolute, unpopular measure.

You are the Prefect, and not a priest in the parish. Is it acceptable for, say, a priest who works with young people to argue or act differently than he would if he were the head of the Congregation for the Doctrine of the Faith?

Yes, of course. In any case, he has to argue and speak differently, otherwise he wouldn't be understood at all by a young person. There is also the rhythm of the generations that has to be respected. The faith is a path on which we have to acknowledge stages. What must keep us together is that we don't pass on private opinions, or simply collective opinions that are current today, but that as believers and priests we connect people with the teaching of the Church and try to transmit it correctly in the given context.

This means that young priests out in the youth ministry who in part have problems proclaiming the sexual morality of the Church as they're supposed to can be forgiven if on occasion they say something that you don't like.

Yes, of course, if the basic intention is there. That is the crucial point. No one unfailingly finds the right means at the first go.

Is a cardinal allowed to talk about sex?

Yes, of course. After all, he has to talk about everything human. And sex is not something to be labeled "sin" and dismissed but is first of all a gift of creation. In my present job, I have to talk a great deal about it. I do try to avoid reducing morality, to say nothing of Christianity, to the sixth commandment, but the insistent questions of the Christian people compel us to deal constantly with this area of human existence.

You once called sex a sort of floating mine and a ubiquitous power. That sounds rather like a negative attitude toward sexuality.

No, that's not the case, for that would be contrary to the faith, which tells us that man is created by God in his totality and that he is created by God as man and woman. So sexuality is not something that originated first after sin but really belongs to God's creative plan. For to create man as male and female means to create him sexually, so that it really belongs to the primordial conception of creation as such and thus to the primordial good of human existence.

If I expressed myself as you cited, I meant that it is indeed the great forces that, when torn away from their human center, can also be the most destructive. Sexuality forms man's entire bodiliness, whether male or female. Precisely because it is great and because man can't become mature without it, can't even become himself, it molds the person most deeply. However, when sexuality escapes man's unity, it can also tear him apart and destroy him.

However, one must admit that this image of sexuality as a ubiquitous power also imposes itself increasingly on us in our day.

Technology and the media have obviously made it possible to tear sex out of the totality of the person and the coexistence [*Miteinander*] of man and woman in a way that wasn't possible earlier. It's now possible really to offer sex in a neutralized form as merchandise.

But that has been the case for two thousand years . . .

Yes, that's true, but the fact that I can directly purchase sex in a shop or that in the corresponding flood of images I can perceive people as nothing more than sex objects, hence, no longer as persons, that has reached a new level through marketing. The possibility of making sex a commodity and of making it available in mass form creates possibilities of alienation, of abuse, that go beyond anything we have been accustomed to until now.

In the Middle Ages there were public brothels that were even in part run by the local Church.

There's a passage in Saint Augustine where he asks what one should do about this problem. And he answers that, given man's makeup, it's better for the order of the commonwealth when prostitution exists in an ordered form. In this respect, one could definitely appeal to the reflections of a great Father of the Church, who was realistic enough to see that man was always tempted and threatened in that area, that whole religions have slid in that direction. But I think that in the meantime there is a specific threat that didn't exist in earlier times.

So is someone who lives strictly in accord with Catholic sexual teaching proof against these temptations?

You can't say that, if only because man is never simply complete but is, as we have observed, always on the way and therefore always at risk. He must become himself anew again and again. He is never simply there. He is always free, and freedom has never reached its conclusion. But I think that someone who is really in a living community of faith in which we support one another, in which mutual support creates encouragement, can also live his marriage well.

In your job, are you afraid of certain questions—perhaps because you won't be able to answer them?

"Afraid" may not be the right word. But we are in fact constantly confronted with problems where it isn't possible to find the right answer in a short time. Above all in the case of problems having to do with ethics, particularly medical ethics, but also in the area of social ethics. For example, the situation in American hospitals forced us to deal with whether it is obligatory to continue giving food and water to the very end to patients in an irreversible coma. This is certainly enormously important for those in positions of responsibility, if only because they are really concerned and because it's necessary to find a common policy for hospitals. We finally had to say, after very long studies, "Answer that for now on the local level; we aren't far enough along to have full certainty about that."

Again in the area of medical ethics, new possibilities, and with them new borderline situations, are constantly arising where it is not immediately evident how to apply principles. We can't simply conjure up certitude. Then we have to say, "Work this through for now among yourselves, so that we gradually mature to certainty from level to level within the context of experience."

But you think there will and must be answers?

There needn't always be universal answers. We also have to realize our limits and to forgo answers where they aren't possible. But, as I said, in the examples cited just now, it simply is not the case that we want to go around giving answers in every situation, but the question really arises, and there is a need for a common direction. However, we don't find answers by forcing everything into a system. Rather, we find them through many such people exposed to borderline situations who know they exercise a common responsibility.

I have not yet completely understood this method, nor do I understand the tools with which one can deal with such complex questions, which certainly are not decreasing in number . . .

On the one hand, there are basic principles. In this case, the principle that man is man from the beginning to the very end; we do not have mastery over human life but have to respect it as something given and have to value its dignity to the very end. So there are certain principles, not many; they are simple but nonetheless essential. Now, new medical and technical capabilities give rise to borderline situations where one asks: How do I apply this principle correctly in this case? Here the first thing needed is information. The doctors have to explain what they can do, what the problems are that arise in this connection.

Let's take the case of water and nourishment. A situation arises in which the patient can no longer be treated medically. At that point, some say that it's an added torture for the patient when food is artificially injected or introduced into his body. Others say, no, it's inhuman, he will die of thirst, and that's the real mistreatment. At first there are two opposing positions on the issue. We must now seek to find out the needed information. Needless to say, a broad acquaintance with doctors is required for that. When the information gradually and to some degree converges, we can ask what corresponds now to the principle and how it is properly applied. But only gradually, when common experiences develop in which, on the one hand, the information is correct and, on the other, the principle is applied correctly can common experience become a statement about what we have to do. Then I can say that the principle is applied correctly in this or that case.

Can ancient texts also be cited for our modern problems? I mean now texts of Church Fathers and saints?

They can be used in the fundamental sense that they shed light on what we were just talking about, namely, the principles regarding the meaning of respect for man and his dignity, the meaning of suffering, but not, of course, for the specific concrete question. They are important inasmuch as our generation, I believe, has lost the sense for the positive side of suffering. And on that score there are really things that we have to relearn.

We were speaking just now of ancient texts. Have you run across secrets in the cellars of the Holy Inquisition; is there something there that will never be divulged?

The "cellars of the Holy Inquisition" are our archives, to give them their right name. We don't have any other cellars. I must confess that I make little use of the archives, simply because I don't have the time to do so. For that reason, I haven't been in a position to stumble upon any special secrets. The fact is that Napoleon confiscated the archives. A part of the contents was subsequently returned, but that's just the point, only a part, so they are certainly no longer complete. And, in general, it is not half so interesting as people expect. A quite liberal Italian professor recently spent some time working on various proceedings and remarked that he was very much disappointed. Instead of the battle between conscience and power that he hoped to run across, he discovered quite ordinary cases of criminal activity. That was due to the fact that the Roman Inquisition was a relatively mild court. So people who faced a civil tribunal falsely accused themselves of some religious offense, such as witchcraft or fortune telling, so that they could appear before the Inquisition, from which they could generally expect a relatively clement judgment. But I know that only secondhand; I haven't studied the matter in the sources.

The exceptional things in the archives are common knowledge; everything else there is more a matter of interest to specialists. There are secrets that can't be disclosed only in the sense that many things were also tried under the seal of confession and thus are protected by the secrecy of the confessional. These things are stored in a separate vault, nor may they be made public.

But if they are protected by the seal of confession, how is it that they exist in written form in the first place?

They weren't confessions in the strict sense, but they are things that are considered as belonging to the inner sphere of conscience and, therefore, are de facto surrounded with the same type of secrecy. I mean it makes a difference whether someone advocates a theological error, about which you can speak publicly, or has deep personal and moral problems.

I assume those aren't the confessional secrets of Tom, Dick, and Harry, but of the powerful people of history?

I know much too little about it. Even today we still have a disciplinary section that deals with certain offenses committed by priests. These offenses are known only in the narrowest circles and, in order to protect the individual, aren't to be revealed to anyone else. These are the sorts of things at issue here.

But aren't famous prophetic secrets also stored in this archive?

Only Fatima, as far as I know. I don't know whether we have any other prophecies.

Who is allowed to examine it?

The Pope himself may examine it, and the Prefect of the Congregation. Others with the Pope's personal approval.

Is the circle of people who have examined these secrets known and easy to keep track of?

It's certainly easy to keep track of. Probably there are no more than three or four people.

You once went so far as to say that the prophecy of Fatima speaks of what "Jesus himself often reminded us of, in that he isn't afraid to say, 'If you don't convert, you will all perish.'" Did the prophecy shake you?

No.

Why not?

Because nowhere does it say anything more than what the Christian message already says.

But doesn't it speak of the destruction of the world?

I can't say anything about that now. In any case, I wasn't overcome by any terrible shocks.

And times and dates?

No. But I don't want to enter into any further details here.

It is sometimes said that Pope John Paul II would be inconceivable without Cardinal Ratzinger, and Cardinal Ratzinger without the Pope. You are considered the brilliant theologian at the side of a philosopher. One never knows, though, what is the Pope's goal and what is Ratzinger's idea. You have been a chief shaper of this pontificate. Without this special Wojtyla-Ratzinger connection, the Church would likely have taken a different course at the end of the millennium.

That's a question I can't answer, of course. But I would caution against overestimating my role. Of course, I have an important task; the Pope trusts me; we've always discussed very important doctrinal matters with each other and continue to do so. In that respect, I've had a say in the Pope's official teaching and contributed something that has also given shape to the pontificate. But the Pope has very much his own course.

For one thing, he had already begun his triptych before I came—the three encyclicals on the Redeemer of Man, on the Holy Spirit, and on the mercy of God. In addition to that, there is the whole sector of social ethics, that is, the three encyclicals he wrote on the Church's social teaching. These are things that have arisen from very deep within his own experience of life, his own philosophy. Also the urgent ecumenical impulse that moves him is something rooted very deeply in his own soul, in his own personality—"rooted" is perhaps too undynamic an expression for the force that works and operates in him. On the other hand, naturally, he has discussed the major questions with me, but not only with me. Here a deep inner harmony emerged. At some point, Christianity and mankind will judge whether they benefitted by this.

Have there been differences between the Pope and his chief guardian of the faith? Have you ever contradicted the Pope or even refused him something?

There have never been differences in the strict sense of the word. Of course, when you are exchanging information, it's possible to correct one another; something is either correct or it is not. It is possible to say, for example, that one's knowledge isn't precise enough. It's also the case that when you attempt to discuss the question, you see a different logic. But there has never been a difference in the true sense. And I have never refused the Pope anything.

How is your collaboration organized practically? Do you see each other very often?

First of all, there's the normal routine. The Prefect of the Congregation normally has an audience with the Pope every Friday evening and presents the results of the regular session of the cardinal members of the Congregation (once a month the Secretary does that, and sometimes the audience is canceled). That's the normal way for our work to be presented to the Pope. The Pope also has the minutes in hand. We discuss the results. Then the Pope decides. In addition, there are meetings that are set for extraordinary situations.

Paul VI had already kept Tuesdays free, and the present Pope has adopted that. He usually uses that time in order to gather a discussion group about an hour or an hour and a half before lunch, which then luncheons with him, so it's possible to discuss with one another from 12 to 3. This occurs with relative regularity and is the second kind of meeting. There the circle is somewhat larger, whereas during the Friday audience the Prefect is alone with the Pope.

The Pope gathers discussion groups whose composition varies according to need. Or else the group may consist, for example, of a whole group of bishops of a country. In these groups, individual persons first briefly present their position. This gives rise to a discussion. In other words, the Pope wants to begin by getting acquainted with the information in order to understand the arguments of both sides where they're different and in order to let the right decision gradually be reached. The two basic levels are, on the one hand, the Friday audience and, on the other hand, these midday discussions where there is an exchange.

Can you give an example of the subjects?

All the matters that have become decisions, beginning with the questions of liberation theology, with the questions about the function of the theologian in the Church, with bioethical questions, and so on. In short, all the themes that are in the competence of the Congregation.

When it is a question of what you could call major projects, the source materials are exchanged at regular intervals. When, for example, an encyclical is being produced, there is a discussion about how to begin approaching it. Then there is a first draft, which is discussed in common. The major subjects are never, as it were, sprung on him but are talked through in several stages. He sees the stages and then also intervenes himself.

Does he also inquire later what has happened with the projects?

If we don't inform him, yes.

As head of a state, the Pope is the last absolute ruler in Europe. As the head of the Church and the successor of the apostles, he is the final authority in matters of faith. The Vatican is considered superannuated. People say that it is a withdrawn, self-sufficient circle of old men that is no longer in touch with the concerns and needs of the communities outside. An example of this would be the proverbial slowness of the Vatican, so that it now lags infinitely behind the times. What kind of picture of the Vatican do you, as an insider, have?

Let's distinguish now the Vatican state, where the Pope is head of state. It's theoretically correct that he alone has all the rights, but de facto he hardly exercises his function as head of state. It is a tiny state in which, however, there are also administrative tasks; for that purpose, there is a so-called *governatorato*. In other words, the Vatican has its own government.

Now, the personnel also have representation, so that governance is not at all carried on in the old-fashioned way that one might expect.

As to the other question, he is the chief guardian of the faith, that is correct, but even here he doesn't make decisions dictatorially, but in a fundamental attentiveness listens to the episcopal college. It is true that the Vatican is characterized by a certain slowness, for the simple reason that so many intermediate bodies have to be traversed, and because it is also required by the duty of accuracy. On the other hand, this slowness is also due to the small staff, and in a place where so many things are going on at once, the progress of individual proceedings can't be accelerated. But I don't consider that a disadvantage. Rather, in something like the government of the Church, hectic activity would be out of place, and patience is really a good instrument. Some questions are settled by letting them take their own course for the time being and by not always stepping in immediately.

It is, of course, true that the circle of cardinals is a circle of old men, or at least of not exactly young men. The advantage is that, in general, decisions aren't rushed, that there is a lot of experience of life there, which can also make one rather forbearing. But it's also necessary to ensure that the element of youth is represented. As a rule the assistants have to be under thirty-five years old when they begin, and then they can't stay on forever, so that these relatively younger assistants also contribute other elements.

It is said that in the Vatican you have to know how the power-plays work and that you also have to learn to play them.

That can well be an aspect of the situation in that some people play career politics and try to be on the right side at the right time, in order to get ahead and to avoid suddenly falling out of favor. There are such things, for the simple reason that we're among human beings. I must say that I know really very little about that. I came in as a cardinal, so I didn't need to play for power or to worry about a career. For that reason, the question doesn't interest me very much either.

Is there something about the Vatican that bothers you?

I do believe that the administration could be somewhat reduced, although I don't have any concrete suggestions about that. The individual offices are not very highly staffed, and in relation to the universal Church as a whole it may not be an excessively large administration. Nevertheless, it is legitimate to ask whether the bureaucracy couldn't be reduced in constructive ways. But on the whole I am very happy with the life in our Congregation. What bothers me personally is really the fact that we are supposed to do too much. For I believe that, realistically, it is hardly possible for anyone to live up to all that is expected. A question that I ask myself is how I can do my duty in the other Congregations as well—and still remain a human being and somehow also keep my personal relationships from disintegrating.

How many Congregations do you belong to?

Five Congregations, two boards, and one commission (Latin America). But only the Congregation for Bishops and the Propaganda require constant work. The demand placed on me by the Council for Unity, the Congregation for the Oriental Churches, and the Congregations for Education and Worship is less regular but still noticeable. But that is already quite a bundle.

Archbishop Marcinkus once spoke of a village of washerwomen, by which he meant the Vatican. "Get three or four priests together, and they start criticizing other people."

That generally doesn't go on in my presence. But it is clear that where so many people live in such close quarters and are involved with each other in so many ways there is also a lot of gossip. Certainly, there is no way to condone that, but in some sense I also see the inevitable limitations of humanity. Here we have to take leave of an overly idealized image of the priest. We must, I think, realize to our salutary shame that we are not so different from everyone else and that the typical laws of social groups turn up even when priests are gathered together. Here each person has to try to work against the tendency. Here, too, we need to allow ourselves to discipline one another. That is a challenge. But I believe it is a very good thing for us to put aside every conceit, to be forced to see that we are really not other people than we are.

Summary

You have never been one for dispensing easy-to-use prescriptions. You have been opposing the trend for decades now. Does not someone in your position also sometimes wonder whether he is acting correctly, whether he is sending the right signals and also whether he has found the mode of expression appropriate to the situation?

One has to ask oneself that in any case. But, thank goodness, there will also be others who can express things differently, who can do what I myself am unable to do. One becomes more modest, one gets to know the limits of one's own capabilities. One sees that what one does is only one contribution alongside of which there have to be completely different ones. And that besides those who reflect and besides those who hold office, there have to be above all the charismatics, those who ignite life. In that sense, I do try to see that what I do has its meaning only within a diverse context and that in this context self-criticism is essential.

If you could take only two books with you to a desert island, you once said, they would be the Bible and the Confessions *of Saint Augustine. What confessions could we expect from Cardinal Ratzinger?*

I don't have any confessions as great as Augustine's to make. In recounting the question of his life and his personal history, he illuminated the whole of Christian existence. I can leave behind modest fragments. Whether that is something that will have continuing significance for humanity or is useful only at the moment, I leave entirely open.

Is there also something that you would undo if you could?

As a matter of fact, I wouldn't undo anything. I would do many things differently now, because at this stage of one's life, one sees some things from a new perspective.

One often has the impression that you have been trying to preserve something, like a father who wants to preserve the inheritance created with so much hard work, if not for his own children, who apparently can't do credit to it or use it, then at least so that his grandchildren can still have access to it and so that it not be squandered. When you look back on your work as Prefect, have you, say, prevented bad developments, even though the public took no notice of that?

I like that idea of preserving something even for one's grandchildren. For what I really have at heart is keeping this precious treasure, the faith, with its power to enlighten, from being lost, and this applies to the good and beautiful things that have accrued to it in our history. I think it is good for this to remain accessible and visible. As far as the balance is concerned, I would say that I do think that with our statements about liberation theology and bioethics and with the *Catechism* we have helped somewhat in the developments of the last fifteen years. Above all, our contacts with the bishops' conferences have led to a greater mutual understanding and have also helped the bishops to a common view of their task, in common among themselves and in common with Rome. In that sense, it has been possible to offset the danger of one-sided emphases, to come back again and again to the essential and to set the right emphases in light of it.

In one of the documents bearing your signature you recalled the admonitions of the Apostle Paul: "Preach the word, be urgent in season and out of season, convince, rebuke, and exhort, be unfailing in patience and in teaching. For the time is coming when people will not endure sound teaching, but having itching ears they will accumulate for themselves teachers to suit their own likings, and will turn away from listening to the truth and wander into myths. As for you, always be steady, endure suffering, do the work of an evangelist, fulfil your ministry" [2 Tim 4:2–5].

I don't want to overreach myself, but I would say that this expresses the essence of what I consider to be my standard at this time.

Do you still have something like the question of all questions? And if you could ask the world-spirit [Weltgeist] something, what would you like to know?

The question that I would have is the one that basically everyone has: Why is the world as it is? What is the meaning of all the suffering in it? Why is evil so powerful in it when God is the one with the real power?

I suspect that there won't be another man of your caliber, with your biography, with your way of thinking, acting, and believing, at the head of the Congregation for the Doctrine of the Faith. With you ends not only a century but also a generation whose roots reach back into the nineteenth century. The "new is already coming", you once said. How do you yourself see your position in history? To what ex-

*tent have you already opened the door to the new? Or will and must
your successor do that?*

I would relativize all that and say that we must wait to see and
will see what figures will come afterward. They will be very
different times; in that respect these figures will have another
form [*Gestalt*]. And concerning one's place in history, we
can't gauge that right now. To be sure, one who has lived in
this century has lived in a time of great transformations and
does in fact reach back in some way into what came before.
In that sense, it's true that there is still a very lively contact
with things that have since disappeared. The fact that we have
been pushed into an entirely different world has also given
rise to the function of maintaining continuity as we proceed.
I have tried to do that. Whether on account of subsequent
historical developments this will later appear to have been a
key position is a question we have to leave entirely open. One
sees, of course, the violent revolutions of one's own lifetime,
but the great perspectives that come after are closed to us.
What fell to me, I think, was to remain in this continuity, to
carry it farther, and, at the same time, to mediate it to an increasingly accelerating history.

*It is commonly conjectured that there are two Ratzingers: one before
Rome, a progressive, and the other in Rome, the conservative and
stern guardian of the faith. So the former theological teenager with
progressive traits becomes a resigned conservative with occasional
apocalyptic moods. You yourself once said that Joseph Ratzinger has
always remained true to himself, whereas the others have moved
away.*

I think I have already made the essential point, namely, that
the basic decision of my life is continuous, that I believe in

God, in Christ, in the Church, and try to orient my life accordingly. This decision unfolds in the process of life, and in that sense I think it's also good that it didn't freeze at some point or another. The ages of life change a man; he shouldn't try to be a seventeen-year-old when he is seventy, and vice versa. I want to be true to what I have recognized as essential and also to remain open to seeing what should change. And what surrounds a man also changes his position. He suddenly finds himself in a different network of coordinates. The framework of discussion in the Church today is completely different from what it was thirty years ago. In this sense, the circumstances give one's words and actions another value. I don't deny that there has been development and change in my life, but I hold firmly that it is a development and change within a fundamental identity and that I, precisely in changing, have tried to remain faithful to what I have always had at heart. Here I agree with Cardinal Newman, who says that to live is to change and that the one who was capable of changing has lived much.

Every task usually demands a price, especially a task so lofty as service to truth.

To serve the truth is a great thing and this vocation's highest purpose. But that is naturally paid out in small coin. That happens in very diverse, very simple and small things, somewhere in the background. The will to truth remains fundamental, but de facto I have to attend to correspondence, read documents, carry on discussions, and so forth.

For me the cost was that I couldn't do full time what I had envisaged for myself, namely, really contributing my thinking and speaking to the great intellectual conversation of our time, by developing an opus of my own. I had to descend to the little and various things pertaining to factual conflicts and events. I had to leave aside a great part of what would interest me and simply serve and to accept that as my task. And I had to free myself from the idea that I absolutely have to write or read this or that. Instead of that, I had to acknowledge that my task is here.

Do you accept your life; are you a happy man?

Yes, I accept it, because to live against oneself and one's life would make no sense. And I think that I have been able to do something meaningful after all, in another way than I had foreseen and expected. And I am really thankful for the life God has disposed and shaped.

Faith, hope, charity, the cardinal virtues—what do they mean in the life of Joseph Cardinal Ratzinger?

We have spoken a great deal about faith. To begin with, it is the root that opens up the basic decision to perceive God, to take God at his word, and to accept him. And that's the key that explains everything else.

This faith implies hope, for the world as it is, is not simply good, nor should it stay that way. If you consider it in purely empirical terms, you could think that evil is the chief power in the world. To have Christian hope means to know about evil and yet to go to meet the future with confidence. The core of faith rests upon accepting being loved by God, and therefore to believe is to say Yes, not only to him, but to creation, to creatures, above all, to men, to try to see the image of God in each person and thereby to become a lover. That's not easy, but the basic Yes, the conviction that God has created men, that he stands behind them, that they aren't simply negative, gives love a reference point that enables it to ground hope on the basis of faith. In this sense, hope contains the element of confidence in the face of our imperilled history, but it has nothing to do with utopia: the object of hope is not the better world of the future but eternal life. The expectation of the better world supports no one, for it's not our world, and everyone has to deal with his world, with his future. The world of the coming generations is essentially molded by the freedom of these generations and can be determined by us in advance only to a very limited extent. But eternal life is indeed my future and thus a power that shapes history.

PART 2

Problems of the Catholic Church

Rome under Fire

Hundreds of thousands of people still come when the Pope says Mass on his journeys, but these huge assemblies can hardly give information about the real state of the Church. As early as 1984, you spoke of a process of decline with respect to the situation of the Church. Now, it seems that soon the Catholic Church will be comparable to the famous black holes in space. In other words, to a collapsing star whose center has long become invisible and gradually shrinks to dwarflike proportions. Its existence is still noticeable, but only in the bewildering movements around its once huge mass. Small fragments of the old mass that aren't able to escape the attraction of the mother-body fly helplessly around in small new units, collide, or destroy one another.

I find very interesting the image of the black holes, of collapsing stars. It can certainly look that way empirically. No mass movement toward faith follows on the process just described in the present phase of history. The historical hour isn't turning around, nor is this star becoming compact again, as it were, or returning to its accustomed size and luminosity. It would undoubtedly be false to expect that a sort of historical shift could take place, that the faith will again become a large-scale mass phenomenon that dominates history.

But I continue to believe, as I always have, that there are also silent revolutions, that the Church is once more, so to speak, reassembling herself from the pagans and that in this sense the experience of Jesus' disciples and of Jesus himself repeats itself. When he says "I have not found such faith in Israel", he credits, as it were, the whole heathen world with stirrings of faith that aren't present with the same degree of vitality among today's Christians. Today's Christians are often weary of their faith and regard it as a very heavy baggage that they drag along but that they aren't really joyful about. In this sense, the image of the star has its limits, because Christianity, as I have already said, finds itself again and again in the position of the mustard seed, but that is also precisely what constantly rejuvenates it. Whether it will again shape history as it did the whole Middle Ages is something no one can predict. But I am quite certain that it will continue to be present anew and in new ways—also as a vital presence in history—once again forming places of survival for mankind.

However, the mere experience of the negative, the knowledge that things are going awry without faith and that we are entering into a huge void, is not of itself sufficient to produce faith. This experience can "peter out" in simple resignation or in total skepticism or in cynicism—or lead to still further destruction of man.

Still, a paradoxical situation has arisen. In the midst of a planetary shift whose pace is hardly tolerable for many people, a basically religion-friendly climate has developed. There is a demand for new intense and hybrid forms of spirituality such as never before. But the hitherto strongest battalions of religion, the Churches of the Christian countries, aren't managing to profit from this general search for meaning.

First of all, it's correct that in a certain respect a new age of religion has dawned. It's true that people are searching in a great variety of ways for religion but don't think that they can find it in the Christian faith, in the Church, but are on the lookout for wholly new forms. However, in these forms, religion is frequently found in a kind of transfigured form whose function is to counterbalance everyday life, or else it slides into magic and cults and then assumes pathological forms. The great Churches of the Christian countries are perhaps also suffocating on account of their own over-institutionalization, of their institutional power, of the pressure of their own history. The living simplicity of the faith has been lost to view in this situation. Being a Christian means simply belonging to a large apparatus and knowing in one way or another that there are countless moral prescriptions and difficult dogmas. Christianity thus appears as traditional and institutional ballast that can't be jettisoned only because there is still some recognition of the ancillary function it performs. But the flame that really enkindles can't, you might say, burn through because of the excess of ash covering it.

There seems to be more than ash covering it. According to the stereotypes of contemporary mainstream opinion, the Roman Catholic Church is not only considered to be a relic of a bygone time that is almost despicable to the world at the end of the second millennium after Christ. There actually seems to be no greater provocation than the mere existence of the official Church. That there is a God, that he has a Son, and that God sent this Son in order to redeem mankind is a fact that sounds for many people in this day and age like the message of a sheer lunatic. One can probably say that hardly any other institution provokes the world more than the Catholic Church—and, strangely, that it provokes even the Western world, which has been shaped by Christian faith and the Church.

In many respects, however, it says something *for* the Catholic Church that she still has the power to provoke, that she is a thorn in the side and a contradiction or, as Saint Paul says, a *skandalon*, a stumbling block. This shows that she means something and that you can't simply pass over her and go about the day's business. Very early on I said that it is necessary to distinguish between the primary and the secondary scandal. The secondary scandal consists in our actual mistakes, defects, and over-institutionalizations, but the primary scandal consists precisely in the fact that we stand in opposition to the decline into the banal and the bourgeois and into false promises. It consists in the fact that we don't simply leave man alone in his self-made ideologies. For this reason I would say that the fact that the Catholic Church is a scandal, insofar as she sets herself in opposition to what appears to be a nascent global ideology and defends primordial values of humanity that can't be fit into this ideology of unity, is in itself a positive one.

What is particularly astonishing is the extent to which the Church has suffered a loss of credibility. A particularly grotesque example: when the Pope, several years ago, pointedly referred to the existence and significance of angels, a lot of people took that as a joke. But suddenly angels have become fashionable. Of course, they are now the right angels, the good ones that apparently have also left the Church.

It really is quite amusing to observe how quickly the intellectual fashions change. At first there was a sort of rationalistic convention that, as it were, wanted to bequeath to the world a Christianity purged of its superfluities. Angels and saints—all that was no longer seemly. Then, suddenly, there comes a new impetus for the mysterious and for a world that, in spite of everything, is still somehow filled with the transcendent. And this includes, in fact, a new "angel craze" that comes to us from outside the Church and is fraught with a lot of dubious things. It should naturally give us pause that statements of faith, when they come from the Church, are either ignored or felt to be repellent, whereas when they come from outside they suddenly regain their urgency. That surely shows that a weariness has crept into the inner life of the Church, a weariness that obscures the beauty and human necessity of matters of faith. In this sense, I think that what is coming from outside can also help us to wake up to ourselves again.

To address once more the extent of what is happening: knowledge about faith is also gone, as if it had all of a sudden been mysteriously vacuumed up by an alien power. In Germany, for example, 30 percent of the people think that Christmas is a fairy tale by the Brothers Grimm. The priests no longer know who they are; the faithful no longer know what they are supposed to believe; the theologians continue to undermine the foundations of tradition. The treasures of the liturgy are being squandered.

You have just made a number of critical remarks that we perhaps ought to examine one by one. If we did so, I would perhaps even have to defend the theologians. But we won't go into those details now.

You are right. There has been a collapse even of simple religious information. This naturally forces us to ask: What is our catechesis doing? What is our school system doing at a time when religious instruction is widespread? I think that it was an error not to pass on more content. Our religion instructors rightly repudiated the idea that religious instruction is only information, and they rightly said that it is something else, that it is more, that the point is to learn life itself, that more has to be conveyed. But that led to the attempt to make people like this style of life, while information and content were neglected. Here, I think, we ought really to be ready for a change, to say that if in this secular world we have religious instruction at all in the schools, we have to assume that we will not be able to convert many in schools to the faith. But the students should find out what Christianity is; they should receive good information in a sympathetic way so that they are stimulated to ask: Is this perhaps something for me?

Today it often seems that those who still attend Mass, take part in processions, and speak positively about the Church are considered by the majority to be a little band of exotics. And even this little remnant must increasingly have the impression that with their Christian ideas they live in a world that no longer has anything to do with the world around them. Isn't the process of decline really in fact more dramatic than one might like to believe?

Certainly, at present Christianity is suffering an enormous loss of meaning, and the form in which the Church is present is also changing. The Christian society that has existed until now is very obviously crumbling. In this respect, the relationship between society and the Church will also continue to change, and it will presumably continue in the direction of a dechristianized form of society. What is happening in the world of faith will no longer automatically have an innovative impact on the general consciousness of society.

The central area of life today is that of economic and technical innovations. There—and in a very special way in the entertainment world of the media as well—language and behavior are shaped. That is, as it were, the central zone of human existence, the zone that is addressed in great mass movements. In this case, religion hasn't disappeared, to be sure, but it has migrated into the realm of subjectivity. Faith is then tolerated as one of the subjective forms of religion, or else it retains a certain space ultimately as a cultural factor.

On the other side, however, Christianity will offer models of

life in new ways and will once again present itself in the waste-
land of technological existence as a place of true humanity.
That is already happening now. I mean, one can always raise
objections to individual movements such as the Neo-
catechumens or the Focolarini, but whatever else you may say,
we can observe innovative things emerging there. In these
movements, Christianity is present as an experience of newness and is suddenly felt by people—who often come from
very far outside—as a chance to live in this century. Hence the
public function of the Church will no longer be the same as it
was with the traditional fusion of Church and society, but it
will still be visible, even publicly, as a new opportunity for man.

*Concepts drawn from the spectrum of the Church, which once spoke a
universal language, no longer play any role today. And the Church is
obviously increasingly losing her creative powers. Almost up to our
days it was taken for granted that artists and intellectuals were also
professed members of the Church. For centuries this was in any case
no problem. Raphael, Michelangelo, Bach, great artists, were im-
mensely creative in their willingness to serve the Church. Today, however, artists engage themselves, if at all, in Greenpeace or Amnesty
International.*

This has to do with the historical process we just described.
The public culture of the present day, represented by the media, is a culture characterized by the absence of transcen-
dence, a culture in which Christianity is not seen as a force
determining the shape of things. Here moral energies seek, in
part, other paths, as you just said. But I am quite sure that the
Church will not lack creative energies even in the future.
Think of late antiquity, where Saint Benedict probably wasn't
noticed at all. He was also a dropout who came from noble
Roman society and did something bizarre, something that

then later turned out to be the "ark on which the West survived". And in this sense, I think that today there are Christians who drop out of this strange consensus of modern existence, who attempt new forms of life. To be sure, they don't receive any public notice, but they are doing something that really points to the future.

Could you describe this "strange consensus of modern existence" in greater detail?

It consists in what I was just alluding to: God doesn't count in man's ethos. Even if he exists, he doesn't have anything to do with us. That is virtually the universal maxim. He doesn't concern himself with us; we don't concern ourselves with him. Consequently, the question of eternal life doesn't count either. Responsibility before God and his judgment is replaced with responsibility before history, before humanity. This gives rise to criteria that are definitely moral and that can be set forth even with considerable fanaticism, for example, the struggle against overpopulation, which is coupled with the general battle to conserve the biological equilibrium. But at the same time this means that everything is allowed that doesn't compete with these. Because there is no authority to answer to apart from public opinion and its tribunals (which can be cruel), the motivational power of these ideals in individual lives is often negligible. The thrust of these ideals tends to benefit more those who are far away rather than those who are nearby. Near at hand, it is frequently egotism that tends to thrive.

On the State of the Church

A universal Church is forced to deal with many chronological dispari-
ties. The cultural and historical differences of individual peoples pro-
duce formidable variations. The Catholic Church doesn't consist of
just the emancipated, critical, authority-weary West. There are also
the martyr Churches of the East, the socio-politicized Churches of
South America. In addition there are many conflicting tendencies of
faith and thought. Today it seems easier to register the differences in
the Church than what is held in common. Is there still a consensus?

Yes. I see that when we consider just the picture of the bishops from around the world. Of course, the circumstances of
dialogue, the temperaments, the ecclesial situations they rep-
resent, are all very different. But there is still the common
catholicity expressed, for example, in the liturgy, in the other
forms of devotion, in the fundamental moral precepts, in the
distinctive convictions that shape us. Even though the
Church has become substantially more multifarious, in her
core she is a Church that expresses herself in the Creed and
also in practice in her union with Rome, which is understood as a link to a common faith-identity. In this sense, while
there is no doubt that very different worlds live side by side,
beyond these great differences they have such a great unity
that at any time we can celebrate Mass with one another, can
speak with one another and understand one another in terms

of basic concepts and elements. I think that the Catholic Church also contributes something important to humanity in that she keeps these worlds together, different as they are, within a basic consensus and thereby also creates bridges from world to world.

Isn't this basic consensus really a minimal consensus?

No, I wouldn't say so. Its form is no longer so crystalline, so uniform, as it perhaps was fifty years ago, or whenever. It has become more diverse culturally. But it has a very solid unity. In other words, everyone reads the same Bible, in the same spirit of the Catholic tradition, and knows that he is committed to the same Creed and the same Magisterium. The realization of this differs according to circumstances, but there is definitely a perceptible unity, which I experience very palpably in meeting with bishops, but also with youth groups from around the world. A specific Catholic identity is something that can be really experienced over and above all barriers.

In addition, one must of course take into account that amid the chronological differences and cultural contrasts there are also worldwide currents of unity and uniformity. Technology and the media also create a climate of world unity. Television penetrates today even into the poorest corners of the world; it broadcasts a certain ideology, and there is hardly any place where technology is still absent. So the conflicting forces today are, on the one hand, a tendency toward uniformity that brings everyone to this same level of world technological achievement and its ideas. On the opposite side, however, is a defense of identity in which cultures are more vigorously resisting this trend toward uniformity and are in quest of their original physiognomy. This shows that the uniformity and reach of the technological global culture, which penetrates everywhere, isn't sufficient to found a deeper unity in humanity, a unity that touches the inner levels of man. Therein lies the more complicated and, in many respects, also much more important situation of the Church.

What do you mean by that?

The convictions and modes of behavior that hold the Church together are located at a deeper level than the forms of expression and behavioral patterns that are imposed on us by the mass media. The operation of a computer, the handling of a car, the use of an assembly line, the construction of a skyscraper, and so forth, are all things that work with slight variations in the same way and by the same technical laws everywhere in the world. But completely different styles of life can be connected with that. The outward doing is the same everywhere, but that doesn't mean that the people doing the same things can understand one another, that they can respect each other and be at peace with one another. Religious and ethical convictions are of decisive importance for that, indeed, the whole method of forming conscience. But that is what the Church is about. It is obvious that this formation of the inner man, which is hardly tangible from the outside, is more difficult and, at the same time, more important for keeping humanity together and for maintaining its human dignity. This makes it easy to understand that a common, sensible expression of the common formation of conscience in a common faith is essential. What doesn't appear externally is ineffectual. For this reason, it is important, for example, for the liturgy, as well as the Church's life as such, to give sensible, tangible form to what is held inwardly in common beyond cultural frontiers.

Is it possible to define basic constellations and fronts, or even perhaps factions, within the Church?

There are, of course, currents that flow around the world. First of all, there is the basic idea of liberation theology. This idea has found an echo on every continent, really, and it must be said, too, that it can be given a very positive expression. After all, its core idea is that Christianity also has to have an outward effect in man's earthly existence. It has to give him freedom of conscience, but it also has to try to vindicate his social rights. However, when this idea is understood one-sidedly, it attempts to conceive of Christianity in general as an instrument for refashioning the world politically. This approach gave rise to the idea that all religions are basically just instruments for advocating freedom, peace, and the conservation of creation, so that they would have to justify their existence through political success and political goals. This thematic varies according to the given political situations, but it cuts right across the continents. Today it has strong roots in Asia but also in Africa. It has, by the way, penetrated even into the Islamic world, where there are attempts to interpret the Koran in terms of liberation theology. Naturally, that remains marginal, but the Islamic terrorist movements have made much of the fact that Islam is really, as they see it, a liberation movement—for example, against Israel.

In the meantime, the idea of liberation—if we may indeed call freedom the common denominator of the modern mind and of our century—has also fused very powerfully with feminist ideology. Woman is now considered the real victim of oppression. Therefore, the liberation of woman is the core of every activity undertaken for the sake of liberation. You might say that, here, political liberation theology has been superseded by an anthropological one. What is meant by libera-

tion in this instance is not simply liberation from imposed social roles but, ultimately, a liberation that aims to free man
from his human biological determination. A distinction is
now drawn between the biological phenomenon of sexuality
and the forms it has taken in history, what one calls "gender".
But the call for revolution against the whole historical shape
of sexuality leads to a revolution against the biological givens
as well. The idea that "nature" has something to say is no
longer admissible; man is to have the liberty to remodel himself at will. He is to be free from all of the prior givens of his
essence. He makes of himself what he wants, and only in this
way is he really "free" and liberated. Behind this approach is a
rebellion on man's part against the limits that he has as a biological being. In the end, it is a revolt against our creatureliness. Man is to be his own creator—a modern, new edition
of the immemorial attempt to be God, to be like God.

The third phenomenon that can be observed around the
world—and this, mind you, in a world of increasing uniformity—is the quest for one's own cultural identity. This is expressed in the concept "inculturation". In Latin America, the
rediscovery of lost cultures has become a powerful current after the ebbing of the Marxist wave. The *teología india* sets out
to reawaken pre-Columbian culture and, so to speak, to get
free of the foreign overlay imposed by Europe. There are interesting cross-connections to feminism here. Much is made
of the cult of mother earth and, in general, of the feminine in
God. This reinforces the tendencies of American-European
feminism, which is no longer content with purely anthropological statements but also intends to recast the concept of
God, since, as it is claimed, patriarchy has been projected
onto God, and the concept of God has accordingly been used
to keep the oppression of women firmly in place. Then there
are points of contact between the cosmic element (mother

earth, and so on) in the renewal of ancient religions and the ideas of New Age, which aims at a fusion of all religions and a new unity of man and cosmos. Back to inculturation, which exists also and especially in Africa and Asia, particularly in India—though, needless to say, in a way proper to each. The question is: To what extent can cultures be used to clothe various religions? Are they merely clothing? Aren't they living wholes? What is culture anyway? There are major issues and tasks in this field.

Then I would mention two additional topics that are making the circuit of the globe. The first is ecology. The idea comes from the awareness that we can't treat the earth as we do. That awareness has subsequently spawned a kind of embarrassment about humanity, about man who, as it were, sucks creation dry, as well as the question of what man is, after all, and whether he shouldn't take his place once more among the other animals, and more of the same. It is possible to have a Christian ecology, because of belief in creation, which sets limits to man's caprice, which places normative criteria before freedom; it is also possible to develop it in an anti-Christian spirit, with a New Age inspiration, starting from the divinity of the cosmos. The other subject I would like to mention is the current of relativism, which has become very strong. It grows out of various roots. For one thing, it seems to modern man undemocratic, intolerant, and also incompatible with the scientist's necessary skepticism to say that we have the truth and that something else is not the truth, or is only fragmentary truth. Precisely this democratic understanding of life and the concomitant idea of toleration has made the question of whether we are entitled to go on with our Christian self-understanding a burning one.

In India this has joined forces with the local religious tradition, which right from the start has characteristically sought

God only in the unnameable. Accordingly, everything religious is just a matter of reflections, copies, refractions of something that never itself appears. Accordingly, there can't be one true religion either. In this context, Christ is, to be sure, a great, towering figure, but we have, as it were, to bring him back down to size, in the awareness that what appears in him has appeared in others too. We have here, in other words, a democratically tolerant world-attitude combined with a great cultural tradition.

How significant or dangerous are these worldwide trends of opinion for the Catholic Church? It does seem today already quite scandalous to the public mind that the Christian faith continues to present itself as the true religion, that it says that Christ is more than a towering figure, that religion is more than a mere human construct.

It seems to me that the questions regarding to what extent it is legitimate to speak of truth at all and how Christianity must fit itself into the universal system of religions have become dramatic in an altogether new way. The center of gravity of this discussion is India, but the problems are also aired in South American theology, via, for example, the *teología india.* In America and Europe it's obviously already very present because of our consciousness of relativity.

How does it stand with those tendencies within the Church that some label as reactionary, as Catholic fundamentalism?

In view of everything that is happening and of the massive uncertainties that are now rising to the surface to threaten man, who suddenly feels bereft of his spiritual homeland, his foundation, there is a reaction of self-defense against, and refusal of, modernity, which as such is conceived of as hostile to religion or, at any rate, hostile to belief. I would, however, add that the catchword "fundamentalism", as it is used today, covers very different realities, and this calls for a bit more precision. The term first arose in nineteenth-century American Protestantism. The historical-critical exegesis of the Bible that had developed in the wake of the Enlightenment took away the univocal meaning that the Bible had had until then and that had been the presupposition of the Protestant scriptural principle. The principle "Scripture alone" suddenly ceased to furnish clear foundations. In the absence of a Magisterium, this was a deadly threat to communion in faith. In addition, there was the theory of evolution, which not only called into question the creation account and belief in creation but rendered God superfluous. The "fundament" was gone. A strictly literal biblical exegesis was set in opposition to this. The literal sense is unshakably valid. This thesis is directed against both the historical-critical method and the Catholic Magisterium, which does not admit this kind of verbalism. This is "fundamentalism" in the original sense. The Protestant fundamentalist "sects" are scoring great missionary successes today in South America and in the Philippines. They give people the feeling of certain, simple faith. Among us, however, fundamentalism has become a household word, a catchword that covers every imaginable foe.

So which currents of fundamentalism, to stay with this expression, do you see more positively, and which do you find dubious or pathological, as you said earlier?

Let's put it this way. The common element in the very diverse currents that are labeled fundamentalism here in the West is the search for a certain and simple faith. That is not bad, as far as it goes, for, in the end, faith—as the New Testament repeatedly tells us—was intended precisely for the simple and the little ones who can't live with complicated academic subtleties. If today living in persevering uncertainty is glorified and faith as a truth that we have found is suspect, this is certainly not the form of life into which the Bible wants to lead us. The quest for certainty and simplicity becomes dangerous when it leads to fanaticism and narrow-mindedness. When reason as such becomes suspect, then faith itself becomes falsified. It becomes a sort of party ideology that no longer has anything to do with turning confidently to God as the primordial ground of our life and reason. It is then that pathological forms of religiosity arise, for example, the quest for apparitions, for messages from the beyond, and the like. But instead of simply hammering away at fundamentalism—whose definition keeps getting broader and broader—theologians should ponder to what extent they are to blame for the fact that increasing numbers of people seek refuge in narrow or unhealthy forms of religion. When one no longer offers anything but questions and doesn't offer any positive way to faith, such flights are inevitable.

Where is the Church still healthiest? Is there a sort of new core Catholic country?

I wouldn't venture to say so. No. On the one hand, there are islands in which traditions are defending themselves more vigorously, and, on the other hand, there are places where the crisis hasn't taken such a radical turn or in which new movements have found a greater response. But faith is in jeopardy everywhere, and that belongs to its nature.

As Prefect of the Congregation for the Doctrine of the Faith and a member of the Congregation for the Evangelization of Peoples, you have a certain overview of the situation. Of course, it is impossible to do justice to the whole range of issues by trying to illuminate the situation of the Church around the world with spotlights, as it were. However, such an approach does, at least, yield a certain impression of the varying topics.

Could we look at the situation in some selected countries, first in Europe, perhaps beginning with Italy? In Italy the characteristics of the Church have always varied a great deal, from the more enlightened Church in the north to the more popular and traditional Church in the south. Now there is obviously a polarization between a progressive and a conservative wing as well as an increasingly powerful influence of the lay movement.

Needless to say, not even Italy has been spared polarizations, but, as far as I can observe, they are less strong than in Germany. Of course, even in Italy theology has adopted critical movements and accentuated them in distinctive ways. The split among the Christian Democrats, which is now complete, indicates more than just divergent schools of politics in Italian Catholicism but gives us a glimpse of deeper theological tensions as well. But the link to the papacy and to the Pope's Magisterium is much more deeply anchored in Italian Catholicism than in ours, and that keeps Italy's Catholics very strongly together despite all the tensions.

It is correct that Catholicism in southern Italy has an entirely different face than in the north. Its style is shaped much more by the heart, by folkloric elements, by traditions and processions. In the north it has a much more pronounced rational and Middle European stamp. And it is correct, as I have already said, that there is quite a considerable range in theology and that critical theologians are by no means lacking, not even in the pontifical universities. But it has never gotten to the point of such radical confrontations as in the north; at some level there is still an attempt to stay together. And it is also part of the Italian consciousness that the Pope in his Magisterium is an essential reference point in the Church.

Of course, the number of churchgoers has dropped in Italy as it has in all the European countries. It is much the same with religious vocations. However, a certain basic Catholic awareness, which, to be sure, is in part very vague, is present among almost all Italians. Even among adherents of the leftist parties, the old Communists. Again and again one sees that in some vague way they understand themselves as Catholics, even when that understanding has few visible effects on their thinking and acting. It's much more a part of Italian identity and culture than, say, in Germany.

Critics say that the Italian Church suffers from a certain weariness, that at present it's mainly cultural projects that are helping the Church to make it through.

Italy is obviously no exception to this weariness, and what you are saying, these evasions, also exist. But there are also very many really vital parishes and very many lay activities in Italy. The insistence on order and normality is perhaps not as extensive as in Germany, but, on the other hand, in my opinion, the spontaneous initiatives are more vigorous and vibrant. For example, the number of candidates for the priesthood in the Diocese of Rome is at present higher than it was fifty years ago.

To what extent has the collapse of the political system also shaken the Italian Church?

In Italy it is always difficult to say to what extent anything has been shaken at all. Political systems collapse, and then nothing

really changes. It's correct that the policy of the Italian episcopal conference had to change. In the final years of the
Democrazia Cristiana, there was a very strong insistence on the
political unity of Catholics, and it was looked upon as a major
goal that Catholics, in accord with their political responsibility, should show their unity in the political sphere as well.
That didn't alter the fact that the *Democrazia Cristiana* subsequently disintegrated, so that the Italian episcopal conference
was obliged to give up this aim. Right now it's withdrawing
to a much greater extent into political neutrality and sees it as
a new aim that Christians in all parties should act "trans-
versely", as they say here, that is, should cross party lines in
the sense of acting harmoniously in terms of their common
responsibility in the essential ethical questions. The goal,
then, is an altogether new political consensus overarching the
parties, a consensus that should develop on the basic ethical
questions.

And would you support this consensus?

Yes, if it succeeds, I would think it very good if there were an
essential unity across party lines.

Even with Communists?

In the post-Communist Democratic Party of the Left, at any
rate, that should be possible. The *Rifondazione comunista* [Com-
munist Refoundation] retains the principles of Marxism, of
course.

*Italy is very different from Germany in the sense that there move-
ments like the "Petition of the People of the Church"* [Kirchen-
volksbegehren] *obviously play no role. Is less attention given to*

dogmatic issues and instead more to social questions having to do
with applied Christianity? What is the difference? What moves the
Italians?

Perhaps one should start by saying that the attempts to start a
"Petition of the People of the Church" aroused practically
no enthusiasm in Belgium and France, and I suspect that
they're having little effect in the United States either. It's
probably a very German phenomenon. Even in Belgium it
required a considerable refashioning of the German "Petition of the People of the Church" to make it interesting. I
don't know how it stands in other countries. In Italy, no one,
in my opinion, would understand the contrast between a
gospel of condemnation [*Drohbotschaft*] and a gospel of affirmation [*Frohbotschaft*], because it makes sense to everyone
that the gospel also has to threaten us with judgment in order to help us in our weakness. Also the fuzzy formula "a
Church of brothers and sisters" probably doesn't say anything to anyone here. People know all too well that siblings
aren't always a model of peaceful coexistence. People know
quite well that celibacy also provokes human problems and
tragedies, but they are realistic enough to know that it's no
easier with marriage. So people still regard celibacy as a bit
of Catholic culture whose importance they recognize despite all potential failures and which they wouldn't want to
see missing. One could continue in the same vein. Italy has
not had a schism in the Church, but it is split into *cattolici* and
laici. By *laici* is meant the champions of a philosophy of the
state and of a conception of life whose great historical expression is the French Revolution. The Freemasons, who as
exemplary *laici* had an essential part in the founding of the
Italian national state, look upon themselves as the torch-
bearers of this world view. The confrontation is between

these two worlds, with the addition of the Communist alternative since the Second World War. The question, then, is principally how to achieve a balance between these three forces, which syntheses are possible or necessary and which have to be rejected.

Let's take a look at Spain.

In Spain the crisis of the end of the Franco regime and of the democratic revolution coincided with the crisis of the post-conciliar period. That caused a great convulsion in the Church in Spain. Up until that time, she had been very much identified with society, indeed, with the state, on account of a certain social order. This was now looked upon as an error. The Church had to detach herself from the social framework; she had to redefine herself. This upheaval also resulted in an abrupt drop in priestly and religious vocations, polarizations in theology, and also highly critical theologies. A very strong reserve of critical Catholicism and also of critical theology has remained intact. There is also a very vital movement under way toward a new catholicity formed by the Council and detached from the old traditions of the state Church.

In France, according to a 1994 survey, 83 percent of believers feel that their duty is to their conscience alone, and supposedly only 1 percent of Catholics still let themselves be guided by the official teaching of the Church.

Yes, in a certain sense France may be the most secularized country in Europe. And the self-assurance of the Gallic spirit has always been a factor of a special kind in the Church. I would question to what extent we are obliged to take such percentages literally. It's correct that French Catholicism also covers a great range and has very critical movements, if you think of the magazine *Golia* or *Témoignage chrétien*. On the other hand, there's also a very strong accentuation of tradition. The Lefebvrite movement, and also traditional movements within the Church, are nowhere stronger than in France. In that sense there is a vast gulf separating the antitheses. But here, too, there are great, vibrant new beginnings and joyful forms of Christian life that don't figure much statistically but are humanly great and have the power to shape the future.

The greatest upheaval at the moment is probably taking place in Eastern Europe, where, after the end of Communism, during which the Church was also a resistance Church, she now apparently has to find a completely new role in society.

I lack exact information in this area, because I am not acquainted, or only scarcely so, with theological movements that would be described as critical. In Hungary, the Bokor movement founded by the Piarist Father Bulány is moving somewhat in this direction. It's a base community that arose out of the experiences of persecution. It first developed a strictly pacifist position as an expression of Christian radicality and has increasingly taken a critical stance toward the bishops whom it classes as belonging to the system. Unfortunately, all the attempts at reconciliation have proved unsuccessful. Instead, the movement has established strong links with the critical, antihierarchical theologies of the West. Members can now belong to any religion they want, as long as they regard the commandment of love as the supreme maxim. In the Czech Republic and Slovakia, critical theology was able to develop up to a certain point around the "clandestine" (underground) priests. But these processes aren't shaping the situation. However, it's plain to everyone that, after the phase of the martyr-Church, it's impossible simply to go back to the previous phase of state Churches and that therefore a free adherence to faith has to develop. It's plain that the Church also has to rethink her relation to society. In that sense, there is probably still a lot of interior struggle going on. But a strong and powerful faith has also remained from the time of suffering, and certain antidotes are still working effectively against certain temptations.

Especially in Poland we can observe phenomena that, in Western Europe at least, have long since become inconceivable. I mean the Church's close association with particular political positions, even down to individual persons.

That's obviously a special problem, about which I don't have precise information either. You must always keep in mind that Poland has a turbulent history behind it and that the real identity factor in all the violent discontinuities, revolutions, and collapses in Polish history has always been Catholicism, which in that respect has amalgamated in an altogether unique way with Polish patriotism and national identity. Even when Poland didn't exist as a state, it continued to be Poland through the Church; through the Church the country stayed together inwardly across the borders of the partitions. In this sense a political factor has accrued to the Church in Poland, one that of course now has to be rethought, re-experienced, and "re-suffered". There are certainly processes of clarification under way that can't be accomplished from one day to the next.

Only English Catholicism seems to be growing stronger. And hasn't England evidently always been the favorite fallen-away child of the Roman Church?

Much of Catholicism remained in Anglicanism, as a matter of fact. In this respect, England and Anglicanism have always maintained an unusual intermediate existence. On the one hand, England separated itself from Rome, distanced itself very resolutely from Rome. One need only recall Hobbes, who said that a state must have religion, and there are especially two kinds of citizens that a state can't afford to have: first, atheists; and second, papists, who are subjects of a foreign potentate. So, on the one hand, there is an abrupt dissociation, but, on the other hand, there is a firm adherence to Catholic tradition. In Anglicanism there have always been vital currents that have strengthened the Catholic inheritance. It has always been split in a curious way between a more Protestant and a more Catholic interpretation. The present crisis also shows this. A new situation has been brought about by two circumstances: the extending of the majority principle to questions of doctrine and the entrusting of doctrinal decisions to the national Churches. Both of these are in themselves nonsensical, because doctrine is either true or not true, which means that it's not a matter to be decided by majorities or by national Churches. The resistance to women's ordination and the conversions to Catholicism can be understood in the light of these two points. But it remains true that the state Church itself is not eager to lose the Catholic element and therefore consciously admits bishops who are not for women's ordination and who provide a sort of refuge for the Catholic part of Anglicanism. A strong Catholic potency has always remained in Anglicanism, and it is becoming very visible again in the present crisis.

In South America new evangelical sects are gathering millions of followers, Catholic faithful are defecting in droves. In the largest Catholic country in the world, Brazil, a real war between the Churches has

broken out, with violent altercations between Catholics and members
of the sects. Is this also a consequence of the failure of liberation theol-
ogy—or just the opposite? Would a boost for liberation theology on
the part of Rome have been able to prevent this development?

On this matter the diagnoses vary a great deal, and we also
lack the empirical information. A great number of observers
say that liberation theology never managed to win over the
social stratum it was concerned about, namely, the very poor.
It was indeed the poor who fled because they felt that what
were, after all, very intellectual promises didn't speak to them
personally. Instead, they felt only the loss of religion's consolation and warmth. Needless to say, the proponents of liberation theology contest that. But there is surely a lot of truth in
it. For the very poor, the prospect of a better world that liberation theology held out to them was too far away. As a result, they remained deeply interested in a religion of the
present, in a religion that would reach into their lives. And it
is precisely in this area that a rush to the sects took place, for
the sects offered the elements that could no longer be found
in a more politicized religious community.

But then there is the opposite accusation that the sects lure
people with money and win them over in an essentially dishonest way, which is probably true in part but by no means
explains the spread of the sects as a whole. The fact is that,
above all, charismatic and Pentecostal Churches are making
headway, but so too are the so-called fundamentalist sects,
which in their own way have a very strict faith. The charismatic, Pentecostal tendency shows that people expect more
spontaneity, more concrete experiences of community in the
Church. Less doctrine, in other words, and more experience,
more immediate joy in the faith instead. The fundamentalist
wave shows that people expect a kind of foundational cer-

tainty of faith that remains as a ground for their lives when everything earthly fails.

On the whole, however, one must say that the stability of the sects is relatively minimal. There are large-scale migrations among sects. The migration from sect to sect is also often only the first stage of abandonment of religion altogether. These developments are, naturally, also connected with the restructuring of society, with increasingly intense urbanization. People leave the country, they live in mass assemblages in the cities, but they do not find there any adequate religion. Groups take care of them that give them not only a religious residence but also a spiritual home. There are, then, multiple causes, and one should avoid making overly simple diagnoses.

In the United States, a large number of bishops intend to answer the Roman Church in the future blow for blow, as they say, with polemical writings of their own.

The number is not large, thirty bishops at most. Then, too, I have spoken with one of the main leaders, and he stressed that they have been completely misinterpreted. We're good Catholics, true to the Pope, he said, we just want to introduce better methods. I have read the writings in question very carefully, and I also said that I was fully in agreement with a whole series of things they mention, whereas I thought other things were rather dubious. I would say that there is no really out-and-out anti-Roman mood in the American episcopal conference. It has a certain breadth, which is also a good thing. There are only a few among them who are perhaps really somewhat extreme. But my impression is, after the fifteen years I have been here, that Rome and the United States have learned to get along much better. On the whole, we have a

very good relationship with the American bishops' conference. It's a conference with great intellectual and religious
capacity, with many outstanding pastors who are making an
important contribution to the development of doctrine in
the universal Church. Its officers visit us here twice each year,
and we have a really cordial relationship.

*Can the Church in North America profit from the religious awaken-
ing that is in the offing there?*

Yes, I think so. Although we ought not to read too much into
certain events and mass demonstrations of Catholicism, they
do show that young people in search of religion feel they can
have a home in the Catholic Church and that also the Pope is
a reference point and a religious leader for them. Tensions
have really eased in the last fifteen years, and there have been
a lot of positive new developments. In America there is not
only a movement of conversions among Anglican priests but
also a completely new relationship to the Evangelicals, who
were formerly the sharpest critics of the Catholic Church. At
the Cairo and Beijing conferences a very interesting closeness
between Evangelicals and Catholics developed, simply because they see that Catholicism doesn't, as they have thought
until now, threaten the Bible and overlay it with some kind of
papal domination, but that it is a guarantee that the Bible be
taken seriously. These new rapprochements won't lead to re-
unions any time soon, but they show that Catholicism is once
again an "American" possibility.

What might be spurring on the new religiosity in America?

There are undoubtedly many factors, which I can't analyze
because I have so little knowledge of America. But there is a

commitment to morality and a desire for religion. In addition, there is a protest against the predominance of modern media culture. Even what Hillary Clinton has said—"Turn off the television, don't put up with it any more"—shows that there is a broad current that says we no longer want simply to submit ourselves to this culture.

Africa. Black Catholics still feel that Rome treats them in a stepmotherly fashion and struggle for recognition. On the continent itself, the Church has problems with the incorporation of African rites and cultural characteristics. Should the playing of drums or dancing, for example, be allowed at Mass? Or how should bigamy be dealt with? Some confess: "I'm a good Catholic, and my three wives are as well." At the same time, a competition has obviously begun with Islam, which is becoming attractive for Africans because they believe it offers a better chance for integrating their traditions.

Africa is a continent of hope, it's said, but also a continent, as we know, with very great problems and tensions. We are ashamed, of course, that Catholic countries like Rwanda and Burundi have now become the scene of the greatest atrocities. In that respect we have to ponder a great deal what we must do to make the gospel more effective in the life of society.

After the African synod and also after the numerous meetings we have had with African bishops, I don't have the sense that Africa feels badly treated by Rome. As a matter of fact, all the Africans are proud to belong to something so grand as the Catholic Church. They are also proud of the fact that they belong to her on an equal footing, that an African bishop and cardinal is the same as an Italian, or Spanish, or American one. Among many there is also a fidelity to Rome that really comes from the heart, a love for the papacy and a joy in being Catholic. When we discuss such questions or theological controversies, the African bishops always tell us that when someone really goes too far, then it's the European, not the African, theologian. Perhaps that's a bit simplistic, but it is true that Europeans are generally behind the negative criticisms. This does not mean that there aren't any real questions; there are, of course. But one can't say that an anti-Roman mood dominates African theology.

You have touched upon two major sectors that are both aspects of inculturation: marriage and liturgy. I believe that in Europe the presentation of the polygamy question is somewhat distorted. It's not a problem of great emotions, but a problem of property law, a social problem. How can the lives of these women be safeguarded? How can their position in society be consolidated? For one doesn't marry for love. Rather, it's two clans that marry, it's an exchange of property. In general, then, the bond of affection is not the problem. The real problem is the question: How can a woman who no longer has a husband and thereby no longer belongs to a fixed association still have her proper place in this society? In other words, it's really a problem of the social structure, and the question is: How can structures be found that highlight monogamy as the basic cell of society? But many African bishops are optimistic about this. I can't make judgments about the details.

In the liturgy there are, on the one hand, enough freedoms to guarantee that African customs and perceptions of life can find their place in it. On the other hand, it is important to prevent the Christian liturgy from becoming too quickly overgrown and to hold on to something of its sobriety. Many Africans see it like this as well. They share our opinion that inculturation shouldn't begin right away with the Eucharist.

Islam is, of course, making great strides in Africa—also through its financial power—and recommends itself as the major religion suited to the Africans. It's clear that Africans have to get beyond their tribal religions, and Islam says, "We are the high religion for Africa, because we don't have a complicated doctrine, and we have a morality that suits you." That is catching on in part, but not universally. Nor must we forget that Islam was at the head of the slave traffic and by no means displayed any great regard for the blacks. And, above all, Islam doesn't make any sort of concessions to inculturation. Islam is Arab, and anyone who becomes Islamic takes on this form of life. There is no inculturation here. For this reason Islam has the problem, as does the Church, for that matter, that one layer of life is Islamic, while underneath the old pagan layer of life continues to exist, so that Islam is, so to speak, only a thin covering over what is the actual way of life. In this sense, the struggle for the religious shape of Africa will continue, and it won't be easy, either.

Asia. It's predicted that the Pacific area will have a major economic and even political importance for the next century. What consequences does that have for the Church?

That is very difficult to predict. Until now, in fact, the Churches, prescinding from the Philippines, haven't succeeded in gaining a foothold in Asia on any large scale. This does not mean that Christianity has remained without significance. It has transformed the existing religions, and its effects reach in diverse ways into the various societies. In Japan there are very few Catholics; the number is constant on the whole. But there is a great interest in Catholic customs and Catholic culture. In this sense Christianity exists as a social reality. Not, of course, in the sense that people make a life-long commitment to it, but it is becoming one of the factors shaping society.

In India the percentages are very small, but the whole neo-Hindu movement, which has also achieved greater significance around the world, has incorporated many elements from Christianity in the latter's more liberal form. And then China still lies before us, untapped. In terms of percentages, Christians are a disappearing minority there too, but they do have a spiritual significance. And the fact that they are taken so seriously by the Communist rulers does show that they see the Christians as a force. But I won't venture to predict what effect that will have in the new role of Asia in the organization of the world.

A new critical situation for the Church is created by the increasing persecution of Christians around the world.

Yes, and it takes different forms. In China, despite certain moves toward tolerance, we still have an oppression of Christianity, above all where it wants to be fully faithful to the Pope. And that applies not only to China but also to a whole series of other countries. Again and again it is part of the Church's destiny to find herself—under the most various kinds of regimes—exposed to persecution. And a new peril is also growing: the development of what you might call a modern world view that regards Christianity or the Catholic faith as an intolerant, antiquated affair unreconcilable with modernity and begins to apply pressure. I believe that this peril is already rather great, even though it still doesn't seem immediate. But the social pressure on the Church essentially to conform to today's accepted standards already exists now.

Is that the same as the persecution of Christians? It does make a difference whether Christians are imprisoned or tortured in dictatorial or Islamic states, or whether they are socially marginalized in the West, doesn't it?

Of course, it is not yet persecution; it would be absurd to apply that expression to this case. But there are indeed areas of life—and not a few—in which, once again, it already takes courage to profess oneself a Christian. Above all there is a growing danger of assimilated forms of Christianity, which society then gladly holds up as humanistic forms of Christianity, as opposed to the alleged fundamentalism of those who don't want to be so streamlined. The danger of a dictatorship of opinion is growing, and anyone who doesn't share the prevailing opinion is excluded, so that even good people no longer dare to stand by such nonconformists. Any future anti-Christian dictatorship would probably be much more subtle than anything we have known until now. It will appear to be friendly to religion, but on the condition that its own models of behavior and thinking not be called into question.

The Situation in Germany

It seems that nowhere is there so much unrest, discord, and apostasy from the old faith as in Germany and the German-speaking countries. The German Church also happens to be the richest in the world, but it has less influence on society than other, poorer Churches in poorer countries. Since the First Vatican Council, more than a hundred years ago, there hasn't been as vociferous a protest against the Pope and the Roman Curia as there is today. What is happening? Do you look at your old homeland with melancholy and concern?

I do look at it with concern, because division within the Church and reluctance to believe are increasing on all sides. On the one hand, there are the modern circles, and we all know that for them every reform is insufficient, that they set themselves against the papacy and papal teaching. But even the others, the "good Catholics", if you want to call them that, find themselves on the whole less and less comfortable in the Church. They no longer feel at home; they suffer and grieve over the fact that now the Church is no longer a place of peace where they can find refuge but is a place of constant conflicts, so that they themselves also become uncertain and begin to protest. And this inner division in the Church, which leads to general displeasure with the Church, to general grief over her, is indeed something that should alarm one. Especially because we are also beginning to see an alarming graying of the Church, for example, as communities of sisters gradually approach their extinction and major new movements that once had a significant role appear increasingly antiquated.

A large part of the population is calling for a sharper separation of Church and state. There is talk of removing the mention of God from the Constitution, of eliminating religious holidays, of ceasing to observe Sunday, and of abolishing the Church tax. Crucifixes in classrooms became a constitutional controversy.

The question of how Church-state relations should best be arranged is one that obviously has to be continually posed anew. As long as there is a consensus in society that the basic values of Christianity are also givens for legislation, it's possible to keep state, Church, and society relatively closely interwoven in a meaningful way that isn't opposed to the freedom of religion. But when convictions no longer stand behind it, too much institutional integration can obviously become dangerous. For this reason, I am not opposed as a matter of principle to a move toward stronger models of separation where this is relevant. On the whole, the Church benefitted by being forced to detach herself from the state Church systems after the First World War. Excessively strong ties were always detrimental to the Church. In that sense, I think the German bishops must consider realistically what forms of Church-state ties really coincide with inner conviction and are thus fruitful and where we are just maintaining positions to which we no longer have a de facto right. Such an appraisal is surely appropriate and necessary.

As to the individual points you mention, I would give very different answers. To have God in the Constitution still seems to me to be something very important, for that isn't the property of a certain Christian confession. If we break away entirely from the reality that there is a standard and a Lord above us, then it becomes necessary to put ideologies in their place or to let everything gradually disintegrate. Bultmann, who was a very critical theologian, once remarked that "An unchristian state is possible, but an atheistic one is not." I believe that, in principle, he is correct. Where no standard exists beyond our own opinions of the moment, arbitrary caprice increasingly reigns, and man degenerates.

The other things, such as the question of the Church tax, are all questions that have to be considered with care and prudence.

An explosive question: What might the answer look like?

I won't venture to comment on that. On the whole, the German Church tax system still enjoys the support, it seems to me, of a pretty broad consensus, because there is recognition of the social services performed by the Churches. Perhaps in the future the path could go in the direction of the Italian system, which, on the one hand, has a much lower rate of assessment but, on the other hand—and this seems important to me—is voluntary. In Italy, everyone is obliged to direct a certain quota of his income—o.8 percent, I think—to a cultural or charitable purpose, which can be the Catholic Church. But one can choose the beneficiaries freely. As a matter of fact, the large majority choose the Catholic Church, but the choice is voluntary.

How did you feel about the Karlsruhe decision?

I was incensed, of course, because the arguments for it were, in my opinion, highly questionable, and because I was and still am convinced that, in spite of everything, there is still much common Christian conviction, so that having this sign in our

schools is really meaningful. I was also indignant in the sense
that I think that the consensus of the majority has to be taken
into account in this matter. In this respect, the decision rested
upon too weak a basis even from the standpoint of democracy.
The reaction has shown that there is still a basic consciousness
that we are Christians in our country. That consciousness varies a great deal from state to state. I have been told that in the
bishops' conference the Bavarian bishops have a different
sense of things than the bishops of Mecklenburg–West
Pomerania, where, as a matter of fact, there haven't been
crosses for a long time, which is also true in large parts of
northern Germany. This also goes to show that it isn't a dogmatic question. But that we should so blithely let this sign,
which still keeps us together, be wrenched from us is something of which I absolutely would not approve. Especially
since the Bavarian constitution still indicates that Christianity
is the basis of education, nor has this been challenged, nor, as
far as I know, has it stirred up any controversy.

*So the Prefect of the Congregation for the Doctrine of the Faith
would say: Leave the crosses in the schools!*

Yes.

*Why must discord flourish in Germany? What kind of country is it;
what kind of spirit or demon holds it captive? Are we perhaps suffering here from a lack of being, which for a long time has been compensated for by doing? Grillparzer once said that God has "no reality for
the Germans. They regard him as their work, not themselves as his."*

I think we should also avoid an excess of German self-
accusation. Countries like France, Spain, Italy, or Great Britain also have their anti-Christian movements, if you will, and

their major inner-church problems. Germany does have, of course, a historical burden all its own, which has grown very heavy since 1933–1945. And the question of what actually happened to our people that something like that could take place is one we must ask with great seriousness.

I think that the virtues of the Germans and their vulnerabilities are very closely connected. On the one hand, we are a people who value discipline, achievement, work, and punctuality, and so we really do get things done, a people who today are once again the strongest economic power in Europe and have the most stable currency. But that leads easily to a certain overrating of oneself and to a one-sided mentality that values only things such as achievement, work, production, what we've produced by ourselves, discipline, and thereby allows many other dimensions of human existence to atrophy. It can also lead time and again to a certain arrogance toward other nations, so that people say that only what is German is really any good, the others are all "sloppy", and so forth. This temptation to self-righteousness, to a one-sided evaluation of things in terms of parameters of productivity, is doubtless a part of German, or, at any rate, of recent German, history, and we have to set ourselves against it.

Apparently not just of more recent German history. Stefan Zweig once tried to portray the German national character and religiosity by defining the differences between Erasmus of Rotterdam and Luther. For, as he writes, "the destiny of the world has seldom chiselled out two such perfectly contrasting men as Erasmus and Luther." The contrast, then, would be between conciliation and fanaticism, reason and passion, culture and primal power, cosmopolitanism and nationalism, evolution and revolution. In Luther we notice the "demagogical, fanatical accent in everything". The pent-up resentments of a whole people, says Zweig, played into the hands of this gifted but fanatical

and unpeaceful man: "Germany's whole consciousness of its nation-
hood, eager to rise up in revolution against everything foreign and
imperial, its hatred of priests, its hatred of foreigners, its dark social
and religious ardor".

The century of the Reformation doubtless gave Germany a
very particular physiognomy and, to a certain degree, also
programmed its future history. The contrast between Erasmus
and Luther I find very interesting, but perhaps the accents are
also distributed a bit unevenly. One mustn't forget, after all,
that Erasmus, being nervous about taking definitive positions,
did have a very different inner make-up from Luther but really
didn't have a clear character—something for which the
Catholic side reproached him very sharply. He tried—"aca-
demically", we would say today—to distance himself from his
own decisions, which at bottom is not right, because by doing
that one evades the drama of being human. In this respect,
Erasmus is not all light and Luther all dark, but both have their
problems. Needless to say, we also have to ask what questionable aspects the Reformation introduced into the German
character—which, of course, in fairness always has to be tied
to the question of what is problematic in us because of Catholicism. I think that this is a very special responsibility of the
ecumenical discussion in Germany. We mustn't conceal the
negative aspects that—along with many positive things—
Luther brought into German history, but this mustn't become
a motive for self-righteousness and one-sided polemics.

It seems that in today's confrontation with the Church, the issue has
less and less to do with the contents of the faith itself, the requirements
of religion. Surprisingly, social problems like poverty, pauperization,
and exploitation aren't at issue, either. You once voiced the suspicion
that too many want the Church to go along with the opinion of the

day, with the bourgeois comfort of modern man, who is drowning in his boredom.

I think that that is the case in a broad segment of people. Perhaps, however, we should expand that a bit and say that, on the whole, even the debate within the Church has become fixated on a couple of subjects, thereby ignoring the major challenges of our time. Wherever you go, wherever a diocesan forum convenes or anything else of the kind takes place, you already know what questions are going to be posed: celibacy, women's ordination, and the remarriage of divorced persons. Those are definitely serious problems. But the Church is, as it were, constantly preoccupied with herself on a couple of fixed points. In the midst of all this, there is too little attention to the fact that 80 percent of the people of this world are non-Christians who are waiting for the gospel, or for whom, at any rate, the gospel is also intended, and that we shouldn't be constantly agonizing over our own questions but should be pondering how we as Christians can express today in this world what we believe and thereby say something to those people.

In the consciousness of the Church, at least in Germany, a massive narrowing has taken place. We look only at ourselves; we are concerned only with ourselves; we lick our wounds; we want to construct a nice Church for ourselves and hardly see any longer that the Church doesn't exist for herself but that we have a word that has something to say to the world and that ought to be heard, a word that could give something. We are too forgetful of our real tasks.

Aren't developments in Germany being treated too indulgently in the Vatican as well? One has the impression that insufficient justice is being done to the explosive nature of these developments.

It's true that the German language has traditionally not had a strong presence in the Curia. The romance languages are known and, more recently, also English; German thus lies somewhat outside the field of observation. On the other hand, there is also a presence of Germany and Germans in Rome that cannot be overlooked. Perhaps it's also difficult in Rome to perceive the full specificity of the German situation because it is often connected with very subtle academic theories that aren't easy to understand for someone who lives in a completely different cultural world. In this respect, it is in fact true that the dialogue with Germany is limping somewhat. But I think that there is always something to be said for reacting slowly. Nevertheless, I do think that the dialogue with the German bishops has to be intensified.

What is the relevance of the crisis that the Church is passing through at the moment? Is this the greatest challenge since the beginning? And what does the crisis of the Church mean for the world? You yourself once declared that the extinction of the Church would unleash a spiritual landslide whose proportions we can hardly imagine.

Regarding the first question: I don't know. It is certainly one of the major challenges. But even in the early Church we had two very serious challenges. The first was gnosticism. A gradual recasting both of worship and of faith into ideologies, into myths and images, was taking place in the Church, and it seemed, without anyone noticing it, to be gradually taking over the whole Church. When one reads these things today, one thinks that on the one side were the Gnostics and on the other side the Church Fathers. But that is not correct. Rather, the two were completely interwoven and had first to be brought gradually to a clarification. There was also a very understandable and inviting attempt to jettison the Old

Testament in order to focus exclusively on Paul. In other words, there were movements of self-discovery that were of the utmost complexity. In addition, there was also at best only a rudimentary central Magisterium that could have intervened effectively in these matters. Consequently, the battle had to be fought through bit by bit on the inside. And Christianity could easily have become something else. That was, I think, a great crisis indeed, and it happened right at the dawn of Christianity, when it still had to form itself.

A second crisis—to be sure, not so serious and large, but nonetheless also an important challenge—was the Arian crisis, when for a time the emperors fully backed Arianism, because it was more compatible with the prevailing mentality. The model was: there is one God, and then there is Christ, who is a godlike being. Everyone could understand that. The whole political apparatus was made available to enforce this idea. Even the bishops caved in one after the other—whole conferences, if you will. Finally, the whole Germanic world became Arian, so that at the time the old world, the Romans, were Catholics, and the New World, the Germans, were Arians. People thought they could easily tell in what direction the new, the future lay, as it were.

I think that the crisis of the sixteenth century was also grave, even though it didn't go so much to the roots, because there remained a common acceptance of the Creed. But the inner confusions of the Church were very great, especially since the Reform also immediately split up into various movements, some of which were very radical.

What we are living through today, looked at from this perspective, is perhaps not the greatest challenge since the beginning of Christianity, but it is one that goes to the roots.

Causes of the Decline

How was it possible for the crisis to become so acute? Please let me first ask for reasons that perhaps are to be sought outside the Church.

Since the Enlightenment, a powerful movement has been under way that looks upon the Church as something antiquated. The more that modern thinking has developed, the more radical the question has become. Even though movements back to the Church began in the nineteenth century, on the whole the mentality continued. What could be warranted scientifically became the highest criterion. But this led to a *diktat* of the so-called modern world view—clearly visible in Bultmann. This world view takes a very dogmatic posture and excludes interventions of God in the world, such as miracles and revelation. Man can indeed have religion, but it lies in the subjective sphere and can therefore have no objective dogmatic contents that are binding on all; in this view, dogma in general seems to contradict man's reason. The Church finds herself in this headwind of history, if you will, and it will also continue to blow in the future.

Nevertheless, the one-sidedness of a radical Enlightenment position naturally also emerges, for a religion that is reduced to the purely subjective no longer has any power to form; it is then only the subject affirming himself. A naked rationality reduced to the natural sciences cannot, in fact, answer the real questions—questions like where do we come from, what am I, what must I do to live properly, what am I here for at all. These questions lie on a different plane of rationality. And they can't simply be entrusted to mere subjectivity or irrationality. This is why the Church will, in the foreseeable future, no longer simply be the form of life of a whole society, why there won't be another Middle Ages, at least not in the near future. It will always be what you could call a complementary movement, if not a countermovement, with respect to the prevailing world view. At the same time, however, it will prove its necessity and its human legitimacy.

Already at the end of the Enlightenment, before the French Revolution, it was said that the Pope, this Dalai Lama of Christianity, had now finally to disappear so that the Age of Reason could begin. As a matter of fact, he did disappear momentarily—into French exile. But the papacy became stronger in the nineteenth century than it had ever been before. And, while it is true that Christianity in the nineteenth century did not experience the energy and form of the Middle Ages, it received something much better in return, namely, great social movements and effects. In this sense, in the future there will continue to be two strong, independent streams and forces, which, however, must also continually attempt to exist together. The new situation of the world makes faith more complicated, and the decision for faith is becoming more personal and more difficult, but this situation can't leave Christianity behind as an antiquated institution.

The Church has new competitors. People compare, consider the alternatives, and seek new havens. Perhaps it was easier for earlier generations to preserve the intensity of their faith for the simple reason that they understood their religion as the tried and true religion of their ancestors, so that there was no longer any need to question it. Today a fundamental reservation has crept into this relationship. A sort of modern worldly dogma has arisen that says that the Church is founded primarily on suppression and power. It says that now that people are enlightened and states are secularized, it is perfectly logical that her fortunes should begin to decline.

I would say two things here. First of all, precisely the experience of repressive systems has shown that the Church, by not conforming to a uniform world view, remains as a counterpole; she is present as a worldwide communion, as a force against repression. The twentieth century has made it plain in a hitherto unknown way that precisely the bond of communion that is the Church is a counterforce against all worldly, political, and economic mechanisms of oppression and uniformization. She gives men a place of freedom and sets a sort of ultimate limit to oppression. The martyrs have always resisted in an exemplary way on behalf of others. That the Church is a basis for freedom is evident in Eastern Europe as well as in China, but also in South America and in Africa. She is a basis for freedom precisely because her form is one of communion, which also includes a common binding commitment. Therefore, when I stand up to a dictatorship, I do so, not just in my own name as a private individual, but in virtue of an inner strength that transcends my own self and my subjectivity.

Now for the second point. There is an ideology that fundamentally traces all existing institutions back to power politics. And this ideology corrupts humanity and also destroys the Church. Here is a very concrete example: If I see the Church only under the aspect of power, then it follows that everyone who doesn't hold an office is ipso facto oppressed. And then the question of, for example, women's ordination, as an issue of power, becomes imperative, for everyone has to be able to have power. I think that this ideology, which suspects that everywhere and always what's at stake is basically power, destroys the feeling of solidarity not only in the Church but also in human life as such. It also produces a totally false point of view, as if power in the Church were an ultimate goal. As if power were the only category for explaining the world and the communion present in it. After all, we are not in the Church in order to exercise power as if we were in some kind of association. If belonging to the Church has any meaning at all, then the meaning can only be that it gives us eternal life, hence, real life, true life as such. Everything else is secondary. If that isn't true, then all "power" in the Church—which then sinks to the level of a mere association—is nothing but an absurd "spectacle". I think we have to escape from this ideology of power and this reduction that derives from Marxist suspicion.

The Church has elaborated a not insignificant quantity of prohibitions, in other words, a sort of traffic code to regulate, as it were, the speed of life. Today's "life-style", on the other hand, signals to us at every intersection, "It's OK, step on the gas." In this whirl of instant bliss, religion, too, is socially respectable only as a dream of happiness without tears, as a mystical enchantment of the soul. Perhaps the Church comes under even heavier fire and isn't profiting from today's spiritual awakening because she makes claims, because she talks about sin and suffering and rectitude of life.

Just one example of this curious state of affairs. When it comes to the state, as soon as crimes begin to multiply and society feels its safety threatened, there is an immediate demand for tougher laws. In relation to the Church, whose laws are moral in nature, the exact opposite happens—there is a demand for further relaxation.

In today's world view, the ideas of autonomy and of anti-authoritarianism, if we can put it like that, have become extremely dominant. As dominant as what we were just talking about, namely, the concept of power. The two terms become the only category that really counts in our social life. The consequences, however, are evident: if the autonomous subject has the last word, then its desires are simply unlimited. It then wants to snatch as much from life as it can get out of it. This is, I think, really a very major problem of life today. People say: Life is basically complicated and short; I want to get as much out of it as possible, and no one has the right to stand in my way. Before all else I have to be able to seize my piece of life, to fulfill myself, and no one has the right to interfere with me. Anyone who would stand in my way is an enemy of my very self.

This world view can also be glimpsed in the background of the documents of Cairo and Beijing [the UN Conference on Population and Development and the UN Conference on Women]. Man is conceived in purely individualistic terms; he is only himself. The relation that is an essential part of him and that is what really first enables him to become himself is taken away from him. This claim to be the ultimate and sole authority over oneself, and the claim to have the right to appropriate as much of life as possible, while no one has the right to stand in the way, is part and parcel of the sense of life on offer to man today. In this sense, the "Thou shalt not"—there are normative criteria to which we must submit—is an encroachment, indeed, an outright attack against which people defend themselves. Ultimately, what is once more at issue is the basic question of questions: How does man find happiness? How does he live rightly? Is it true that man can be happy only if he himself is his own norm?

Not long ago I mentioned in a conversation with friends

that here in the area around Frascati they are preparing to prune the grapevines and that they bear fruit only if they are pruned once a year, that pruning is a condition of fruitfulness. In the light of the Gospel, of John 15, that's immediately clear to us as a parable of human existence and of the communion of the Church. If the courage to prune is lacking, only leaves still grow. Applied to the Church: there is only paper, whereas no more life is brought forth. But let's say it with the words of Christ, who tells us: At the very moment when you think you have to possess yourself and defend yourself, precisely then you ruin yourself. Because you are not built as an island whose only foundation is itself. Rather, you are built for love, and therefore for giving, for renunciation, for the pruning of yourself. Only if you give yourself, if you lose yourself, as Christ puts it, will you be able to live.

This basic option has to stand out in all its starkness. It is offered to man's freedom. But it should still really be made plain that to live by making one's own claims is a false recipe for life. The refusal of suffering and the refusal of creatureliness, hence, of being held to a standard, is ultimately the refusal of love itself, and that ruins man. For it is precisely his submitting himself to a claim and allowing himself to be pruned that enables him to mature and bear fruit.

More and more frequently we observe that young people are underchallenged. In fact, the increasing membership in sects with radical internal demands can be partly explained by the fact that, first, young people are looking for certainty, they want a secure shelter, but then also they want to be challenged. Somewhere deep down man knows: I have to be challenged, and I have to learn to form myself according to a higher standard and to give myself and to lose myself.

The discrepancy between faith and society probably stems also from

the fact that society today wants to examine the Church, the history
of the Church and the doctrine of the Church, in terms of a certain
plausibility. But is this approach so wrong?

It's not wrong when one tries to find a certain reasonability
in the faith. After all, that has been a part of the Christian
message since the beginning. The only way the faith could
enter into the world was as a missionary faith, because it was
something that could be understood and that could also be
made evident to people. Paul could speak in the synagogue
not only with the Jews but also with the so-called "god-
fearing", that is, with the pagans who had recognized the true
God in Israel's monotheism. He used arguments to show
them the reasonableness of the claim that only with Christ
did Judaism and the monotheistic heathendom touched by
Judaism reach their full logical conclusion. In this respect,
Christianity's attempt to show the reasonableness of its answers is quite essential. However, when one conceives the
term plausibility so narrowly that one accepts only those
things about Christianity that suit our way of living at the
moment, then, of course, we make Christianity too cheap
and at that very moment are no longer worth anything.

The Mistakes of the Church

Cardinal König once portrayed the situation of the Church in the world today in these terms: "At bottom, we are dealing with a centuries-long development that has led to an estrangement of the Church and the world. There is a growing discrepancy between the state of consciousness of modern man and of Christian teaching." And then he goes on to say: "However, it is also up to the Church, in order to overcome this disturbance in communication, to question herself critically, asking to what extent she is responsible for it."

The disturbance in communication of which Cardinal König speaks is very apparent, and I think there is certainly a partial responsibility on our side. For one thing, we can't find the language for expressing ourselves in the contemporary consciousness. We may come back to terms like original sin, redemption, atonement, sin, and so forth. These are all words that express a truth, but in today's language they don't amount to much for most people. To make their meaning communicable again is doubtless a task to which we should be devoting our efforts. However, that can succeed only if we ourselves live these things interiorly. When they become comprehensible again in new ways by being lived, they can also be stated in new ways. I must add that the communication of Christian realities is never merely intellectual communication. It says something that embraces the *whole* man and that I can grasp only when I enter into the pilgrim community. In this sense, there are two requirements: really to live it and so to come to understand it oneself, and then to create new possibilities of expression through a convincing community that, as it were, ratifies it.

The public image of the Church is in many respects that of a threatening, ossified tribunal. Why is the official Church so severe? As protectress of the flock, mustn't she struggle for souls in a more motherly way?

It's correct that for many people what remains of the Church's words are just a few moral prohibitions—principally having to do with sexual ethics—and in this respect they have the impression that the Church's real function is only to condemn and to restrict life. Perhaps too much has been said and too often in this direction—and without the necessary connection of truth and love. To some extent, it also has to do, I think, with the media's selective way of reporting things. Such prohibitions are interesting as news items; they have, as it were, a tangible content. On the other hand, talk of God, of Christ, and of so many central matters of faith cannot enter into the secular sphere at all, which takes no notice of it. In this respect, one must also ask how the Church herself, instead of simply scolding the media, can properly adapt her public presentation. In the inner life of faith, where the real core of the faith is proclaimed, individual elements can be correctly related to one another, and in that case such prohibitions could have their proper place in a much larger and positive whole. To want to make everything as public as possible distorts, you might say, the proportions. The Church has to consider how to establish the right proportion between internal proclamation, which expresses a common structure of faith, and how she speaks to the world, where only part of what she says will be understood.

The public very often has the impression that the Church just reacts, that she pins her hopes on perseverance, that she points rigidly to divine commandments and for the rest trusts that God will not let his Church go under. There is dynamism all around, but the Church seems incapable of changing her logic and sticks to stubborn self-assertion. She therefore doesn't seem particularly radical, either, but rather rigid, walled-in like a fortress. The message remains mere words.

That obviously varies greatly from culture to culture. When the Church was suppressed under Communist regimes, not only believers but also unbelievers or seekers, such as, for example, Václav Havel, had a different impression. Then there was a real perception of the fact that the Church proclaims the message of freedom. That she offers counterweights. That she is a force that has something to give to nonbelievers, too, and that inspires confidence that totalitarian powers will never wholly win the day.

In Africa, too, where the Church confronts the state and corruption, which is, as you know, the great problem of the African states, the impression that the Church's existence is mainly a matter of stubborn self-assertion is not the predominant one. Rather, people have the impression that the Church is definitely a dynamic force, a force that also defends the Third World, that also takes initiatives on its behalf, that doesn't simply engage in a certain type of purely material developmental aid but really fosters a living exchange. In South America, too, the impression is very different. So whether or not the Church is perceived primarily as really dynamic depends very much on whom you are speaking about. The fact that in Germany, in Central Europe, she appears only as the foe of progress and as a self-defensive institution rests, I think, on an opposite problem, on our own defensiveness, which refuses to tolerate the Church's objection to many things that are comfortable and to our liking.

Don't conform yourselves to the world, demands the Pope. But hasn't the Church conformed herself too much? She seems fixated on securing her own hereditary fiefs; she invests a lot of money, time, and energy in the upkeep of her real estate. Mustn't she, instead of that, make clear once more what her offer of salvation consists in?

I would agree with you there. Even in the Church inertia is a very powerful factor. Consequently, once the Church has acquired some good or position, she inclines to defend it. The capacity for self-moderation and self-pruning is not adequately developed. I think that this is true also and especially of us in Germany, where we have far more Church institutions than we can imbue with ecclesial spirit. And it's precisely the fact that the Church clings to the institutional structure when nothing really stands behind it any longer that brings the Church into disrepute. The impression thus develops that in a hospital or, for example, in a school, people would be committed to act in accord with the Church only because the Church is the owner and has the say. Here there really must be an examination of conscience. Unfortunately, however, it has always been the case in history that not even the Church has had the capacity to reject earthly possession on her own; rather, her possessions have had to be taken away from her again and again, and this forcible removal then turned out to be for her salvation.

Occasionally, however, it has gone somewhat differently. I am thinking of the separation of state and Church in France under Pius X, at the beginning of this century. At that time the Church was offered a formula for retaining her possessions, but it would have involved a certain integration of the Church into state superintendence. On that point Pius X declared that the *good* of the Church is more important than her *goods*. We'll give the goods away because we must defend the good. That, I think, is a great statement, which we must constantly keep in mind.

I am asking myself why the Church isn't better able to convey the faith to us clueless Christian illiterates, why she doesn't more frequently call to mind the greatness of Catholicism, freedom of thought, reconciliation, and mercy. I also miss her traditional rites, her customs, her feasts, which, after all, she could celebrate with pride and with a skill garnered from two thousand years of experience. In a book by Isaac Singer I found the description of a traditional Jewish feast of the tabernacles. There the Rabbi sang the table prayer and preached. The Chassidim were enthusiastic because they had never heard such an interpretation of the Torah. The Rabbi had unveiled holy mysteries. In the evening a festal cloth was finally spread over the table, and then they put a loaf of bread on it and placed a carafe filled with wine and a kaddish cup next to it. The participants had the impression that the tabernacle changed into one of the mansions in the house of God. What happens instead among us is that Christian celebrations turn into civil holidays with sausage and beer.

This, of course, addresses again the topic of the fusion of Christianity and society and the incorporation of Christian elements into customs and feasts, a topic we have already discussed. But I would like to look at another subject in this context. The Rabbi surely said nothing new, but the rite, celebrated faithfully and festively, really makes it new each time and makes it a new presence.

In our form of the liturgy there is a tendency that, in my opinion, is false, namely, the complete "inculturation" of the liturgy into the contemporary world. The liturgy is thus supposed to be shortened; and everything that is supposedly unintelligible should be removed from it; it should, basically, be transposed down to an even "flatter" language. But this is a thoroughgoing misunderstanding of the essence of the liturgy and of liturgical celebration. For in the liturgy one doesn't grasp what's going on in a simply rational way, as I understand a lecture, for example, but in a manifold way, with all the senses, and by being drawn into a celebration that isn't invented by some commission but that, as it were, comes to me from the depths of the millennia and, ultimately, of eternity.

When Judaism lost the temple, it clung to the synagogal feasts and rites and was held together by celebrating the great holy days as rites of the believing household. There is a certain form of shared life in the rites, in which what counts is not pure surface intelligibility but what expresses the great continuity of the history of faith that, as it were, presents itself as an authority that does not come from the individual. The priest is, in fact, not a showmaster who invents something new and skillfully communicates it. On the contrary, he can entirely lack any talents of a showmaster, because he represents something completely different, and it doesn't depend on him.

Of course, intelligibility is also an element of the liturgy, and for this reason the Word of God must be well read, interpreted, and explained. But there are other ways of understanding in addition to the intelligibility of the word. Above all, it is not something that new commissions think up again and again. When that happens, the liturgy becomes something we construct, whether the commissions meet in Rome,

Trier, or Paris. Instead of this, liturgy must really have its great continuity, protected from what is arbitrary, in which I really meet the millennia and through them eternity and am raised up into a communion of celebration that is something other than what commissions or liturgy committees devise.

I believe that a sort of clericalism has arisen here that also makes it easier for me to understand the demand for women's ordination. Importance is attributed to the *person* of the priest; he must be able to handle things skillfully and to be able to present everything well. He is the real center of the celebration. In consequence, one has to say: Why only this sort of person? When, on the contrary, he withdraws completely and simply presents things through his believing action, then the action no longer circles around him. Rather, he steps aside, and something greater comes into view. In this sense I think it's necessary to see much more the impact and power of the tradition that can't be manipulated. Its beauty and greatness touch even those who can't digest and understand all its details rationally. In the center, of course, is the word that is preached and explained.

Wouldn't it be conceivable to reactivate the old rite in order to work against this leveling [Gleichmacherei] *and demystification?*

That alone would not be a solution. I am of the opinion, to be sure, that the old rite should be granted much more generously to all those who desire it. It's impossible to see what could be dangerous or unacceptable about that. A community is calling its very being into question when it suddenly declares that what until now was its holiest and highest possession is strictly forbidden and when it makes the longing for it seem downright indecent. Can it be trusted any more about anything else? Won't it proscribe again tomorrow what it prescribes today? But a simple return to the old way would not, as I have said, be a solution. Our culture has changed so radically in the last thirty years that a liturgy celebrated exclusively in Latin would bring with it an experience of foreignness that many could not cope with. What we need is a new liturgical education, especially of priests. It must once again become clear that liturgical scholarship doesn't exist in order to produce constantly new models, though that may be all right for the auto industry. It exists in order to introduce us into feast and celebration, to make man capable of the mystery. Here we ought to learn not just from the Eastern Church but from all the religions of the world, which all know that liturgy is something other than the invention of texts and rites, that it lives precisely from what is beyond manipulation. Young people have a very strong sense of this. Centers in which the liturgy is celebrated reverently and nobly without nonsense attract, even if one doesn't understand every word. We need such centers to set an example. Unfortunately, in Germany tolerance for bizarre tinkering is almost unlimited, whereas tolerance for the old liturgy is practically nonexistent. We are surely on the wrong path in that regard.

The crisis of the Church—is it possible to pinpoint when it started? Is it the consequence of mistakes from the past? Has the Church also accumulated too much ballast, too many debts for which she now must pay the bill?

On the one hand, there is a historical continuum that we can't escape. Just as our German history is burdened with every sort of good and evil and concerns every generation, the history of the Church is also a factor. One must ask: What are the burdens, the errors, that we have to confess and acknowledge? But along with that there is also the newness of each living generation.

So, though the crisis does have its roots and the conditions that made it possible in the past, I wouldn't go too far in finding distant historical origins. After all, new historical constellations also lead to new high or low points. I always give the following example. When political liberalism was flourishing, there was also a battle against modernism carried on with great severity by Pius X. After the First World War it was suddenly over. Today many say that the problems ought to have been talked through rather than suppressed. But the reality is that the First World War was perceived as the shipwreck of liberalism, which thus disappeared for a time as an intellectually dominant force. Thus, at that time a whole new state of consciousness unexpectedly arose. Not only in Catholicism but also in Protestant Christianity. Harnack, the great master of liberal theology, retired, and Karl Barth with his radical new piety took his place; Erik Peterson, the great Lutheran exegete and historian, converted to Catholicism. A new liturgical movement arose in the Lutheran Church, where previously liberal theology had been decidedly anticultic. This meant, in other words, that in a completely different generational situation, the problems of modernism were no longer of interest. One can find a very apt illustration in the autobiography of Romano Guardini, who was still in his studies during this liberal phase and then came to a consciously antiliberal decision.

After the Second World War, this situation continued for a short time, but very soon an affluent world developed that went far beyond even the *belle époque*. It developed through a sort of neoliberalism, and suddenly Christianity appeared even more retrograde, perverse, and anachronistic than in the situation before the First World War.

In this sense, we have to consider the signs of crisis also in terms of historical epochs. On this score, I think Karl Marx is right up to a point in saying that the ideological constitution of an epoch is always also a reflection of its whole economic and social structure.

Is it possible that in today's process of the Church's decline there are also powerful forces of self-purification at work?

Forces of self-purification are at work, of that I am convinced. But of course one must not facilely conceive of the loss of faith and weariness of faith in themselves as processes of self-purification. The situation offers an opportunity, which, however, can be used in many different ways. Here we also come back to the question of the Church's possessions and institutions. It can lead to purification. However, a purification does not take place automatically, simply because things decline.

It's certainly difficult to measure the Church by her success, least of all according to political or economic criteria, on the basis of turnovers or of membership statistics. Nevertheless, Christ spoke of stewards to whom the Lord entrusted his goods. They were to cultivate and multiply them—even by unorthodox means, by the way.

The first question is: How do we interpret parables correctly? The fact that Jesus takes the story from the sphere of banking, from business transactions whereby one increases the wealth he began with, shouldn't be regarded as a lesson about methods. Even the business of the unjust steward—a particularly difficult parable—where he says, "All right, at least he solved his problem, be shrewd like he was", doesn't mean that one should use dishonest means. It no doubt means that we ought also to be shrewd and alert and take advantage of opportunities; that some things require imagination and creativity. And it certainly means that it's not enough, in order to remain a "good Christian" oneself, to say, I am religious; I find happiness in my own way; what other people do doesn't concern me. Rather, faith is in reality a gift to be passed on, which you don't even really have if you want to keep it for yourself. A Christianity that has really been accepted interiorly comes with the dynamic requirement to communicate. I have found out, so to speak, how to do things right—and so I can't say that's enough for me. For at that very moment I destroy what I have found. It's exactly like when you are filled with joy about something, you have to express it and communicate it in some way, otherwise it's not an authentic joy at all. The fact is, then, that the dynamism of passing on the gift is an essential component of the mission that Christ gave his followers; and even the encouragement to imagination and boldness, even with the risk of losing something in the bargain. In this sense we can't calmly sit down and say, "Well, there's no promise of large numbers; success isn't one of the names of God; we've done our part, and we'll see who comes and who doesn't." This inner restlessness that comes from knowing we have a gift that is meant for humanity must always be present in the Church.

On the other hand, we also have the words "I am sending you like sheep among wolves", and "You will be persecuted." This means, in other words, that we have been told in advance that our work will always be bound up with the destiny of Christ. And I believe that Christians have to live this tension. There must be no self-satisfaction, in the sense that we say, "We have come this far; we can't do any more." Rather, the task of being good stewards is put before us ever anew, that is, of being people who multiply, as Christ said, and, on the other hand, never have success completely in hand.

The Canon of Criticism

*Referring to criticism of the Church, you once spoke of a classical
"canon of issues": women's ordination, contraception, celibacy, the
remarriage of divorced persons. This list is from 1984. The "Petition of
the People of the Church" of 1995 in Austria, Germany, and Swit-
zerland shows that this canon of issues hasn't changed one iota. The
discussion seems to be going wearyingly in circles. Perhaps a few clarifications would help get beyond this impasse. It seems to me that
many don't know exactly what they're talking about when they
speak of the papacy and priesthood, that they actually don't know the
meaning of these terms.*

I would stress again that all of these are certainly genuine issues, but I also believe that we go astray when we raise them
to *the* standard questions and make them the only concerns of
Christianity. There is a very simple reflection that argues
against this (which, by the way, Johann Baptist Metz has mentioned in an article on the "Petition of the People of the
Church"). These issues are resolved in Lutheran Christianity.
On these points it has taken the other path, and it is quite
plain that it hasn't thereby solved the problem of being a
Christian in today's world and that the problem of Christianity, the effort of being a Christian, remains just as dramatic as
before. Metz, if I recall correctly, asks why we ought to make

ourselves a clone of Protestant Christianity. It is actually a good thing, he says, that the experiment was made. For it shows that being Christian today does not stand or fall on these questions. That the resolution of these matters doesn't make the gospel more attractive or being Christian any easier. It does not even achieve the agreement that will better hold the Church together. I believe we should finally be clear on this point, that the Church is not suffering on account of these questions.

The Dogma of Infallibility

Let us begin, then, with a point that the Protestants crossed off the list quite early on, the dogma of infallibility. Now, what does this dogma really mean? Is it correctly or falsely translated when we assume that everything the Holy Father says is automatically sacred and correct? I would like to put this question at the beginning of the canon of criticism because it seems especially to agitate people, for whatever reasons.

You have in fact touched upon an error. As a matter of fact, this dogma does not mean that everything the Pope says is infallible. It simply means that in Christianity, at any rate, as Catholics believe, there is a final decision-making authority. That ultimately there can be binding decisions about essential issues and that we can be certain that they correctly interpret the heritage of Christ. In one form or another this obligatoriness is present in every Christian faith community, only it is not associated with the Pope.

For the Orthodox Church, too, it is clear that conciliar decisions are infallible in the sense that I can be confident that here the inheritance of Christ is correctly interpreted; this is our common faith. It's not necessary for each person, as it were, to distill it and extract it from the Bible anew; rather, the Church has been given the possibility of reaching communal certainty. The difference from Orthodoxy is only that Roman Christianity recognizes another level of assurance in addition to the ecumenical council, namely, the successor of Peter, who can likewise provide this assurance. The Pope is of course bound to certain conditions in this matter, conditions that guarantee—and in addition put him under the deepest obligation—that he doesn't decide out of his own subjective consciousness but in the great communion of the tradition.

It did take a long time, though, to find this solution.

Well, councils were also held before there was any theory of councils. The Fathers of the Council of Nicaea, the first council, which was held in 325, didn't have any idea what a council was; in fact it was the emperor who had convoked it. Nevertheless, they were already clear that not only they themselves had spoken but that they were entitled to say (what the council of the apostles also says) "It has seemed good to the Holy Spirit and to us" (Acts 15:28). This means: the Holy Spirit has decided with us and through us. The Council of Nicaea then speaks of three primatial sees in the Church, namely, Rome, Antioch, and Alexandria, thus naming jurisdictions connected with the Petrine tradition. Rome and Antioch are the episcopal sees of Saint Peter, and Alexandria, as Mark's see, was, as it were, tied to the Petrine tradition and assumed into this triad.

Very early on the bishops of Rome knew clearly that they were in this Petrine tradition and that, together with the responsibility, they also had the promise that helped them to live up to it. This subsequently became very clear in the Arian crisis, when Rome was the only authority that could face up to the emperor. The bishop of Rome, who naturally has to listen to the whole Church and does not creatively produce the faith himself, has a function that is in continuity with the promise to Peter. To be sure, only in 1870 was it then given its definitive conceptual formulation.

Perhaps we ought also to note that in our day an understanding is awakening even outside Catholic Christianity that a guarantor of unity is necessary for the whole. This has emerged in the dialogue with the Anglicans, for example. The Anglicans are ready to acknowledge, as it were, providential guidance in tying the tradition of primacy to Rome, without wanting to refer the promise to Peter directly to the Pope. Even in other parts of Protestant Christianity there is an acknowledgment that Christianity ought to have a spokesman who can express it in person. And also the Orthodox Church has voices that criticize the disintegration of the Church into autocephalies (national Churches) and instead of this regard recourse to the Petrine principle as meaningful. That is not an acknowledgment of the Roman dogma, but convergences are becoming increasingly clear.

The Gospel: Affirmation or Condemnation?

The traditional morality of the Church, according to one criticism, is really based on guilt feelings. It is above all negative in its evaluation of sexuality. The Church, it is said, has also imposed burdens that have nothing to do with revelation. Now there is the idea that we ought to cease basing Christian theology on sin and contrition. It is necessary and possible, they say, to rediscover the mystery of religious experience beyond religious norms.

The sloganlike opposition between "condemnation" and "affirmation" [*Droh-Botschaft/Froh-Botschaft*: threatening news/ good news] is one that I have never thought highly of. For whoever reads the Gospel sees that Christ preached the good news but that precisely the message of judgment is a part of it. There are quite dramatic words of judgment in the Gospel that can really make one shudder. We ought not to stifle them. The Lord himself in the Gospel obviously sees no contradiction between the message of judgment and the good news. On the contrary. That there is a judgment, that there is justice, at least for the oppressed, for those who are unjustly treated, that is the real hope and in that sense good news. Those who belong to the oppressors and the workers of injustice are primarily the ones who feel threatened.

Even Adorno said that there can really be justice only if there is a resurrection of the dead, so that past wrongs can be settled retroactively, as it were. There must, in other words, somewhere, somehow be a settling of injustices, the victory of justice; that is what we are awaiting, at least. Nor are Christ and his judgment a victory for evil. No, *He* is the victory of the good, and, in this sense, the fact that God is righteous and is the judge is profoundly good news. Naturally, this good news puts me under an obligation. But when I conceive of the good news only as self-affirmation, in the final analysis it is meaningless; there is an anesthetization going on somewhere. For this reason we must become familiar again with the dimension of judgment precisely with a view to those who suffer and those who have received no justice but who have a right to it—and then also agree to put ourselves under this standard and to try not to belong to the doers of injustice.

Of course, there is an unsettling element in the message of judgment, and that is a good thing. I mean, when you see how the medieval rulers committed injustice but then, when judgment was approaching, tried to make amends by benefactions and good deeds, you see that consciousness of judgment was also a political and social factor. The awareness that I really mustn't leave the world in this state, that I have to put things right somehow, in other words, that there was an even higher threat hanging over the powerful, was extremely salutary. That benefits everyone concretely.

However, we have to add that we know that as judge Christ is not a cold legalist but that he is familiar with grace and that ultimately we may approach him without fear. But I think that everyone must find this inner balance, must feel that he is under judgment and recognize: I can't simply muddle along as I please, there is a judgment over me—without, however, surrendering to scruples and anxiety.

This, it seems to me, also suggests an orientation for the Church's preaching and pastoral ministry. She must also be able to threaten the powerful; she must also be able to threaten those who neglect, squander, even destroy their lives, for the sake of the right and the good and their own well-being, their own happiness. But she must not become a power that instills fear; she must also know with whom she is speaking. There are sensitive, almost sick souls, who are quickly plunged into fear. They have to be retrieved from the zone of fear; the word of grace has to shine very powerfully into the soul. I believe that both aspects must be kept together in a whole, but in such a way that judgment is also good news, because it assures us that the world makes sense and good triumphs.

We Are the People of God

The term "people of God" is understood today as the idea of an autonomy vis-à-vis the official Church. The motto is "we are the people", and what the people says has to be done. On the other hand, there is also the expression "vox populi, vox Dei". How do you understand this term?

If we are theologians and believers, we listen first to what the Bible says. In other words, we ourselves can't invent the major concepts: "Who is God?" "What is the Church?" "grace", and so forth. The gift of faith consists precisely in the fact that there is a prior given. The term "people of God" is a biblical one. The biblical use is thus also normative for how we might use it. It is first and essentially an Old Testament term; the term "people" comes long before the era of nations and is connected more with the clan, with the family.

Above all it is a relational term. More recent exegesis has made this very clear. Israel is not the people of God when it acts simply as a political nation. It becomes the people of God by turning to God. It is the people of God only in relation, in turning to God, and in Israel turning to God consists in submission to the Torah. In this sense, the idea of "people of God" in the Old Testament includes, first, the election of Israel by God, who chooses it for no merit of its own, despite the fact that it is not a great or significant people but one of the smallest of the peoples, who chooses it out of love and thus bestows his love upon it. Second, it includes the acceptance of this love, and concretely this means submission to the Torah. Only in this submission, which places Israel in relation to God, is it the people of God.

In the New Testament, the concept "people of God" (with perhaps one or two exceptions) refers only to Israel, that is, to the people of the Old Covenant. It is not a concept that applies directly to the Church. However, the Church is understood as the continuation of Israel, although Christians don't descend directly from Abraham and thus actually don't belong to this people. They enter into it, says the New Testament, by their descent from Christ and thereby also become children of Abraham. Thus, whoever belongs to Christ belongs to the people of God. One could say that the term "Torah" is replaced by the person of Christ, and, in this sense, the "people of God" category, though not applied directly to the new people, is tied to communion with Christ and to living like Christ and with Christ, or, as Saint Paul says, "hav[ing] the mind of Christ" (Phil 2:5). Paul goes on to describe the "mind of Christ" with the words: "*He* became obedient unto death on the cross." Only when we understand the term "people of God" in its biblical usage do we use it in a Christian way. Everything else is an extra-Christian construction that misses the real core and is, in my opinion, also a product of arrogance. Which of us can say that we are the people of God, while the others perhaps are not.

But regarding the statement "we are the people" I would add a very practical consideration. The "we are the people" functions as the premise for the conclusion "we decide." If, for example, in Germany all the members of a certain association got together and said, "We are the people, and therefore we decide that now it is thus and so", all the people would just laugh. Every nation has its institutions; everyone knows that it's not the town council but the parliament, in other words, an institution that really represents the whole, that votes on federal laws. And in this way not just anyone is the comprehensive "we" of the Church with the corresponding authority to make decisions, but only everyone together is this "we", and the individual group is this "we" only insofar as it lives in the whole. It would, in fact, be completely absurd even on the purely popular understanding of democracy if groups pretended to vote about the whole themselves. A parish council or a diocesan forum should take in hand *its* affairs. But it cannot claim to decide the affairs of the universal Church as such.

In the Church, there is another element in addition to the example given us by the law of the state (which also has significance for the Church), namely, the fact that the Church lives not only synchronically but diachronically as well. This means that it is always all—even the dead—who live and are the whole Church, that it is always all who must be considered in any majority in the Church. In the state, for example, one day we have the Reagan administration, and the next day the Clinton administration, and whoever comes next always throws out what his predecessor did and said; we always begin again from scratch. That's not the way it is in the Church. The Church lives her life precisely from the identity of all the generations, from their identity that overarches time, and her real majority is made up of the saints. Every generation tries to join the ranks of the saints, and each makes its contribution. But it can do that only by accepting this great continuity and entering into it in a living way.

But of course there is also a continuity of the state that is independent of individual presidents.

Correct. What I said just now was a bit exaggerated. It's also the case in the state that not every government starts all over again from the beginning. Each of them is in the great tradition of the state and, being bound to the constitution, can't reconstruct the state from zero, as it were. So what holds for a state holds also for the Church, only in an even stricter and more far-reaching way.

Now, there are "we are the people" movements that no longer group themselves around the traditional laws, rules, parliaments, but simply go off on their own.

In the state, you mean? Yes, yes. In that sense, the phenomenon is also nothing peculiar to the Church. But these popular democratic movements show us that this really doesn't work in the state. The Soviet Union began like that. The "base" was supposed to decide things via the councils; all were supposed to take an active part in governing. This allegedly direct democracy, dubbed "people's democracy", which was contrasted with representative (parliamentary) democracy, became, in reality, simply a lie. It would be no different in a Church made up of such councils.

The slogan "we are the people" is also attractive because in our most recent past it proved to be successful in the protest movements in the former East Germany.

That's quite true. But in that case the people obviously stood behind it. By now, the consensus has fallen apart again. It was sufficient for a great protest, but it's not enough for the positive task of governing a commonwealth.

Sacred Rule and Brotherhood

Why must the Church continue to operate even today with authoritarian methods and be organized according to "totalitarian" structures? Many people have the idea that democratic models could be possible in the Church, too. It's argued that you can't sue for democracy and human rights in society and then leave them at the door of your own house. You can't go around demanding a sense of fellowship and then operate yourself predominantly with accusations of guilt, laws, and a pointing finger.

First, to the word "hierarchy". The correct translation of this term is probably not "sacred rule" but "sacred origin". The word *archē* can mean both things, origin and rule. But the likelier meaning is "sacred origin". In other words, it communicates itself in virtue of an origin, and the power of this origin, which is sacred, is, as it were, the ever-new beginning of every generation in the Church. It doesn't live by the mere continuum of generations but by the presence of the ever-new source itself, which communicates itself unceasingly through the sacraments. That, I think, is an important, different way of looking at things: the category that corresponds to the priesthood is not that of rule. On the contrary, the priesthood has to be a conduit and a making present of a beginning and has to make itself available for this task. When priesthood, episcopacy, and papacy are understood essentially in terms of rule, then things are truly wrong and distorted.

We know from the Gospels that the disciples argued about their rank, that the temptation to turn discipleship into lordship was there from the first and also always is there. Therefore, there is no denying that this temptation exists in every generation, including today's. At the same time, however, there is the gesture of the Lord, who washes the feet of his disciples and thereby makes them fit to sit at table with him, with God himself. When he makes this gesture, it is as if he were saying: "This is what I mean by priesthood. If you don't like that, then you are no priests." Or, as he says to the mother of the Zebedees: The prior condition is drinking the cup, that is, suffering with Christ. Whether they then sit at the right or at the left or anywhere else, that has to remain open. So that this is another way of saying that to be a disciple means to drink the chalice, to enter into a communion of destiny with the Lord, to wash another's feet, to lead the way in suffering, to share another's suffering. This, then, is the first point, namely, that the origin of hierarchy, in any event its true meaning, is not to construct a structure of domination but to keep something present that doesn't come from the individual. No one can forgive sins on his own initiative; no one can communicate the Holy Spirit on his own initiative;

no one can transform bread into the presence of Christ or keep him present on his own initiative. In this sense, one has to perform a service in which the Church doesn't become a self-governing business but draws her life again and again anew from her origin.

A second general preliminary remark. The word "brotherhood" is, to be sure, a fine word, but we oughtn't to forget its ambiguity. The first pair of brothers in the history of the world were, according to the Bible, Cain and Abel, and the one murdered the other. And that is an idea that also occurs elsewhere in the history of religions. The mythology surrounding the origin of Rome has the same thing: Romulus and Remus. It also begins with two brothers, and one murders the other. So, siblings are not automatically the quintessence of love and equality. Just as fatherhood can turn into tyranny, we also have sufficient examples of negative brotherhood in history. Even brotherhood must be redeemed, as it were, and pass through the Cross in order to find its proper form.

Now to the practical questions. Perhaps there really is too much decision making and administration in the Church at the present time. In reality, office by nature ought to be a service to ensure that the sacraments are celebrated, that Christ can come in, and that the Word of God is proclaimed. Everything else is only ordered to that. It ought not to be a standing governing function but have a bond of obedience to the origin and a bond to the life lived in this origin. The officeholder ought to accept responsibility for the fact that he does not proclaim and produce things himself but is a conduit for the Other and thereby ought to step back himself—we have already touched on that. In this sense, he should be in the very first place one who obeys, who does not say, "I would like to say this now", but asks what Christ says and what our faith is and submits to that. And in the second place he ought to be one who serves, who is available to the people and who, in following Christ, keeps himself ready to wash their feet. In Saint Augustine this is marvelously illustrated. We have already spoken of the fact that he was really constantly busy with trivial affairs, with footwashing, and that he was ready to spend his great life for the little things, if you will, but in the knowledge that he wasn't squandering it by doing so. That would, then, be the true image of the priesthood. When it is lived *correctly*, it cannot mean finally getting one's hands on the levers of power but, rather, renouncing one's own life project in order to give oneself over to service.

Part of that, of course—and here I am citing Augustine again—is to reprimand and to rebuke and, thereby, to cause problems for oneself. Augustine illustrates this in a homily in the following terms: *You* want to live badly; you want to perish. *I*, however, am not allowed to want this; I have to rebuke you, even though it displeases you. He then uses the example of the father with sleeping sickness whose son keeps waking him up, because that is the only chance of his being cured. But the father says: Let me sleep, I'm dead tired. And the son says: No, I'm not allowed to let you sleep. And that, he says, is precisely the function of a bishop. I am not permitted to let you sleep. I know that you would like to sleep, but that is precisely what I may not allow. And in this sense the Church must also raise her index finger and become irksome. But in all this it must remain perceptible that the Church is not interested in harassing people but that she herself is animated by the restless desire for the good. I must not allow you to sleep, because sleep would be deadly. And in the exercise of this authority she must also take Christ's suffering upon herself. What—let's put it in a purely human way—gives Christ credibility is, in fact, that he suffered. And that is also the credibility of the Church. For this reason she also becomes most credible where she has martyrs and confessors. And where things go comfortably, she loses credibility.

Celibacy

Curiously, nothing enrages people more than the question of celibacy. Even though it concerns directly only a tiny fraction of the people in the Church. Why is there celibacy?

It arises from a saying of Christ. There are, Christ says, those who give up marriage for the sake of the kingdom of heaven and bear testimony to the kingdom of heaven with their whole existence. Very early on the Church came to the conviction that to be a priest means to give this testimony to the kingdom of heaven. In this regard, it could fall back analogously to an Old Testament parallel of another nature. Israel marches into the land. Each of the eleven tribes gets its land, its territory. Only the tribe of Levi, the priestly tribe, doesn't get an inheritance; its inheritance is God alone. This means in practical terms that its members live on the cult offerings and not, like the other tribes, from the cultivation of land. The essential point is that they have no property. In Psalm 16 we read, You are my assigned portion; I have drawn you as my lot; God is my land. This figure, that is, the fact that in the Old Testament the priestly tribe is landless and, as it were, lives on God—and thereby also really bears witness to him—was later translated, on the basis of Jesus' words, to this: The land where the priest lives is God.

We have such difficulty understanding this renunciation today because the relationship to marriage and children has clearly shifted. To have to die without children was once synonymous with a useless life: the echoes of my own life die away, and I am completely dead. If I have children, then I continue to live in them; it's a sort of immortality through posterity. For this reason the ultimate condition of life is to have posterity and thereby to remain in the land of the living.

The renunciation of marriage and family is thus to be understood in terms of this vision: I renounce what, humanly speaking, is not only the most normal but also the most important thing. I forego bringing forth further life on the tree of life, and I live in the faith that my land is really God—and so I make it easier for others, also, to believe that there is a kingdom of heaven. I bear witness to Jesus Christ, to the gospel, not only with words, but also with this specific mode of existence, and I place my life in this form at his disposal.

In this sense, celibacy has a christological and an apostolic meaning at the same time. The point is not simply to save time—so I then have a little bit more time at my disposal because I am not a father of a family. That would be too primitive and pragmatic a way to see things. The point is really an existence that stakes everything on God and leaves out precisely the one thing that normally makes a human existence fulfilled with a promising future.

On the other hand, it's certainly not a dogma. Couldn't the question perhaps be negotiated one day in the direction of a free choice between a celibate and a noncelibate form of life?

No, it's certainly not a dogma. It is an accustomed way of life that evolved very early in the Church on good biblical grounds. Recent studies show that celibacy goes back much farther than the usually acknowledged canonical sources would indicate, back to the second century. In the East, too, it was much more widespread than we have been able to realize up until now. In the East it isn't until the seventh century that there is a parting of the ways. Today as before, monasticism in the East is still the foundation that sustains the priesthood and the hierarchy. In that sense, celibacy also has a very major significance in the East.

It is not a dogma. It is a form of life that has grown up in the Church and that naturally always brings with it the danger of a fall. When one aims so high, there are failures. I think that what provokes people today against celibacy is that they see how many priests really aren't inwardly in agreement with it and either live it hypocritically, badly, not at all, or only live it in a tortured way. So people say . . .

. . . it ruins them . . .

The poorer an age is in faith, the more frequent the falls. This robs celibacy of its credibility and obscures the real point of it. People need to get straight in their minds that times of crisis for celibacy are always times of crisis for marriage as well. For, as a matter of fact, today we are experiencing not only violations of celibacy; marriage itself is becoming increasingly fragile as the basis of our society. In the legislation of Western nations we see how it is increasingly placed on the same level as other forms and is thereby largely "dissolved" as a legal form. Nor is the hard work needed really to live marriage negligible. Put in practical terms, after the abolition of celibacy we would only have a different kind of problem with divorced priests. That is not unknown in the Protestant Churches. In this sense, we see, of course, that the lofty forms of human existence involve great risks.

The conclusion that I would draw from this, however, is not that we should now say, "We can't do it anymore", but that we must learn again to believe. And that we must also be even more careful in the selection of candidates for the priesthood. The point is that someone ought really to accept it freely and not say, well now, I would like to become a priest, so I'll put up with this. Or: Well then, I'm not interested in girls anyway, so I'll go along with celibacy. That is not a basis to start from. The candidate for the priesthood has to recognize the faith as a force in his life, and he must know that he can live celibacy only in faith. Then celibacy can also become again a testimony that says something to people and that also gives them the courage to marry. The two institutions are interconnected. If fidelity in the one is no longer possible, the other no longer exists: one fidelity sustains the other.

Is that a conjecture when you say that there is a connection between the crisis of celibacy and the crisis of marriage?

That seems quite apparent to me. In both cases the question of a definitive life decision is at the center of one's own personality: Am I already able, let's say at age twenty-five, to arrange my whole life? Is that something appropriate for man at all? Is it possible to see it through and in doing so to grow and mature in a living way—or must I not rather keep myself constantly open for new possibilities? Basically, then, the question is posed thus: Does the possibility of a definitive choice belong in the central sphere of man's existence as an essential component? In deciding his form of life, can he commit himself to a definitive bond? I would say two things. He can do so only if he is really anchored in his faith. Second, only then does he also reach the full form of human love and human maturity. Anything less than monogamous marriage is too little for man.

But if the figures about the breakdowns of celibacy are correct, then celibacy collapsed de facto a long time ago. To say it again: Is this question perhaps one day negotiable in the sense of a free choice?

The point is that, in any case, it has to be free. It's even necessary to confirm by an oath before ordination one's free consent and desire. In this sense, I always have a bad feeling when it's said afterward that it was a compulsory celibacy and that it was imposed on us. That goes against one's word given at the beginning. It's very important that in the education of priests we see to it that this oath is taken seriously. This is the first point. The second is that where there is living faith, and in the measure in which a Church lives faith, the strength to do this is also given.

I think that giving up this condition basically improves nothing; rather, it glosses over a crisis of faith. Naturally, it is a tragedy for a Church when many lead a more or less double life. Unfortunately, this is not the first time that has happened. In the late Middle Ages we had a similar situation, which was also one of the factors that caused the Reformation. That is a tragic event indeed that calls for reflection, also for the sake of the people, who also really suffer deeply. But I think that, according to the findings of the last synod of bishops, it is the conviction of the great majority of bishops that the real question is the crisis of faith and that we won't get better and more priests by this "uncoupling" but will only gloss over a crisis of faith and falsely obtain solutions in a superficial way.

Back to my question: Do you think that perhaps one day priests will be able to decide freely between celibate and noncelibate life?

I understood your question. I simply had to make it clear that in any event, at least according to what every priest says before his ordination, celibacy is not a matter of compulsion. Someone is accepted as a priest only when he does it of his own accord. And that is now the question, of course: How deeply do priesthood and celibacy belong together? And is not the wish to have only one [without the other] a lower view of the priesthood? Nor do I think that in this matter it's enough simply to point to the Orthodox Churches and Protestant Christianity. Protestant Christianity has per se a completely different understanding of office: it is a function, it is a ministry coming out of the community, but it is not a sacrament in the same sense; it is not priesthood in this proper sense. In the Orthodox Churches we have, on the one hand, the full form of the priesthood, the priest monks, who alone can become bishops. Alongside them are the "people's priests", who, if they want to marry, must marry before ordination but who exercise little pastoral care but are really only liturgical ministers. This is also a somewhat different conception of priesthood. We, on the other hand, are of the opinion that everyone who is a priest at all must be so in the way that the bishop is and that there cannot be such a division.

One ought not to declare that any custom of the Church's life, no matter how deeply anchored and well founded, is wholly absolute. To be sure, the Church will have to ask herself the question again and again; she has now done so in two synods. But I think that given the whole history of Western Christianity and the inner vision that lies at the basis of the whole, the Church should not believe that she will easily gain much by resorting to this uncoupling; rather in any case she will lose if she does so.

Can one say, then, that you do not believe that one day the Catholic Church will have married priests?

At least not in the foreseeable future. To be quite honest, I must say that we do have married priests, who came to us as converts from the Anglican Church or from various Protestant communities. In exceptional cases, then, it is possible, but they are just that—exceptional situations. And I think that these will also remain exceptional cases in the future.

Mustn't celibacy be dropped for the simple reason that otherwise the Church won't get any more priests?

I don't think that the argument is really sound. The question of priestly vocations has many aspects. It has, first of all, to do with the number of children. If today the average number of children is 1.5, the question of possible priests takes on a very different form from what it was in ages when families were considerably larger. And there are also very different expectations in families. Today we are experiencing that the main obstacles to the priesthood often come from parents. They have very different expectations for their children. That is the first point. The second point is that the number of active Christians is much smaller, which means, of course, that the selection pool has become much smaller. Looked at relative to the number of children and the number of those who are believing churchgoers, the number of priestly vocations has probably not decreased at all. In this sense, one has to take the proportion into account. The first question, then, is: Are there believers? And only then comes the second question: Are priests coming from them?

Contraception

Your Eminence, many Christians do not understand the Church's position on contraception. Do you understand that they don't understand it?

Yes, I can understand that quite well; the question is really complicated. In today's troubled world, where the number of children cannot be very high given living conditions and so many other factors, it's very easy to understand. In this matter, we ought to look less at the casuistry of individual cases and more at the major objectives that the Church has in mind.

I think that it's a question of three major basic options. The first and most fundamental is to insist on the value of the child in society. In this area, in fact, there has been a remarkable change. Whereas in the simple societies of the past up to the nineteenth century, the blessing of children was regarded as *the* blessing, today children are conceived of almost as a threat. People think that they rob us of a place for the future, they threaten our own space, and so forth. In this matter a primary objective is to recover the original, true view that the child, the new human being, is a blessing. That by giving life we also receive it ourselves and that going out of ourselves and accepting the blessing of creation are good for man.

The second is that today we find ourselves before a separation of sexuality from procreation such as was not known earlier, and this makes it all the more necessary not to lose sight of the inner connection between the two.

Meanwhile, even representatives of the sixties' generation, who tried it, are making some astonishing statements. Or perhaps that's just what we should expect. Rainer Langhans, for example, who once explored "orgasmic sexuality" in his communes, now proclaims that "the pill severed sexuality from the soul and led people into a blind alley." Langhans complains that now there "is no longer any giving, no longer any devoted dedication". "The highest" aspect of sexuality, he now professes, is "parenthood", which he calls "collaboration in God's plan".

It really is true that increasingly we have the development of two completely separated realities. In Huxley's famous futuristic novel *Brave New World*, we see a vision of a coming world in which sexuality is something completely detached from procreation. He had good reason to expect this, and its human tragedy is fully explored. In this world, children are planned and produced in a laboratory in a regulated fashion. Now, that is clearly an intentional caricature, but, like all caricatures, it does bring something to the fore: that the child is going to be something that tends to be planned and made, that he lies completely under the control of reason, as it were. And that signals the self-destruction of man. Children become products in which we want to express ourselves; they are fully robbed in advance of their own life's projects. And sexuality once again becomes something replaceable. And, of course, in all this the relationship of man and woman is also lost. The developments are plain to see.

In the question of contraception, precisely such basic options are at stake. The Church wants to keep man human. For the third option in this context is that we cannot resolve great moral problems simply with techniques, with chemistry, but must solve them morally, with a life-style. It is, I think—independently now of contraception—one of our great perils that we want to master even the human condition with technology, that we have forgotten that there are primordial human problems that are not susceptible of technological solutions but that demand a certain life-style and certain life decisions. I would say that in the question of contraception we ought to look more at these basic options in which the Church is leading a struggle for man. The point of the Church's objections is to underscore this battle. The way these objections are formulated is perhaps not always completely felicitous, but what is at stake are such major cardinal points of human existence.

The question remains whether you can reproach someone, say a couple who already have several children, for not having a positive attitude toward children.

No, of course not, and that shouldn't happen, either.

But must these people nevertheless have the idea that they are living in some sort of sin if they . . .

I would say that those are questions that ought to be discussed with one's spiritual director, with one's priest, because they can't be projected into the abstract.

Abortion

The Church, says the Pope, will continue her vehement opposition to all measures that "in any way promote abortion, sterilization, and contraception". Such measures wound, he says, the dignity of man as an image of God and thereby undermine the basis of society. The fundamental issue is the protection of life. On the other hand, why is the death penalty, as the Catechism *says, "not excluded as a right of the state"?*

In the death penalty, when it is legitimately applied, someone is punished who has been proved guilty of the most serious crimes and who also represents a threat to the peace of society. In other words, a guilty person is punished. In the case of abortion, on the other hand, the death penalty is inflicted on someone who is absolutely innocent. And those are two completely different things that you cannot compare with one another.

It is true that the unborn child is regarded by not a few people as an unjust aggressor who narrows the scope of my life, who forces his way into my life, and whom I must kill as an unjust attacker. But that is nothing less than the vision we spoke of earlier in which the child is no longer considered a distinct creature of God, created in the image of God with his own right to life, but, at least as long as he is yet unborn, suddenly appears as a foe or as an inconvenience I can do with as I please. I think that the point is to clarify the awareness that a conceived child is a human being, an individual.

That the child, though needing the protection of the mother's bodily communion, is still a distinct person in his own right, and that he must be treated as a human being because he is a human being. I think that if we give up the principle that every man as man is under God's protection, that as a man he is beyond the reach of our arbitrary will, we really do forsake the foundation of human rights.

But can one then say that someone who finds herself in a great moral dilemma and decides to terminate pregnancy is a conspirator against life?

How guilt is assigned to individual persons is always a question that cannot be decided abstractly. But let's say that the act itself—whoever has brought about the situation; it can also be due to pressure from men—remains by its nature an attempt to resolve a conflict situation by killing a human being. We also know from psychology how deeply something like this can stick in the mother's psyche, because she knows at some level that there was a human being in her, that it would have been her child, and that it might have turned out to be someone she would have been proud of. Needless to say, society must also help to ensure the availability of other possibilities for dealing with difficult situations and to end pressure on expectant mothers and to reawaken a new love for children.

Divorced and Remarried Persons

Excommunication in the case of married people who divorce and live in a new civil marriage not recognized by the Church is something that today probably only especially loyal Catholics can agree with. It seems unjust, humiliating, and, in the end, unchristian as well. You yourself observed in 1972: "Marriage is a sacrament . . . this does not rule out that the Church's communion also embraces those people who recognize this doctrine and this principle of life but are in an exceptionally difficult situation in which they especially need full communion with the body of the Lord."

First of all, I must make a purely canonical clarification, namely, that these married people are not excommunicated in the formal sense. Excommunication is a whole cluster of ecclesiastical penalties; it is a restriction of Church membership. This ecclesiastical penalty is not imposed on them, even though what you might call the core that immediately catches the eye, the fact of not being able to receive Communion, does affect them. But, as I said, they are not excommunicated in the juridical sense. They are, indeed, members of the Church who, because of a specific situation in their lives, cannot go to Communion. It is beyond doubt that this is a great burden especially in our world, in which the percentage of broken marriages is increasing.

I think that this burden can be carried if it becomes clear that there are also other people who may not receive Communion. The real reason why the problem has become so dramatic is that Communion has become a sort of social rite and that one is really stigmatized if one doesn't participate in it. If it becomes plain again that many people should be saying to themselves: I've got a few things to answer for, I can't go up to Communion as I am now; and if, as Saint Paul puts

it, the discernment of the body of Christ is once more prac-
ticed in this way, the situation will immediately take on a different look. That is one condition. The second is that they
have to feel that, in spite of everything, they are accepted by
the Church, that the Church suffers with them.

But that sounds like a pious wish.

Of course, that would have to find some expression in the life
of a community. And, conversely, by taking this renunciation
upon oneself, one does something for the Church and for
humanity, in that one bears a kind of witness to the unique-
ness of marriage. I think that this in turn also has a very important aspect, namely, the recognition that suffering and
renunciation can be something positive and that we have
to find a new appreciation for these things. And finally, that
we also recover the awareness that one can meaningfully and
fruitfully participate in the celebration of the Mass, of the
Eucharist, without going to Communion each time. So, it
remains a difficult matter, but I think that when a few connected factors get straightened out again, this will also become easier to bear.

*Still, the priest does say the words, "Happy are those who are called
to the Lord's supper." Consequently, the others ought to feel that they
are unhappy.*

Unfortunately, this has been somewhat obscured by the translation. The words do not refer directly to the Eucharist. They
are, in fact, taken from the Book of Revelation and refer to
the invitation to the eternal marriage feast that is represented
in the Eucharist. Therefore, someone who cannot receive
Communion at the moment is not necessarily excluded from

the eternal wedding feast. There has to be, as it were, a constant examination of conscience. I have to think about being fit for this eternal meal and communicate now so that that actually happens. Even someone who cannot receive Communion now is, like all the others, exhorted by this call to think while he is on the way that he will one day be admitted to the eternal marriage banquet. And perhaps, because he has suffered, that he can be even more acceptable.

Is discussion of this question still open, or is it already decided and settled once and for all?

The principles have been decided, but factual questions, individual questions, are of course always possible. For example, perhaps in the future there could also be an extrajudicial determination that the first marriage did not exist. This could perhaps be ascertained locally by experienced pastors. Such juridical developments, which can make things less complicated, are conceivable. But the principle that marriage is indissoluble and that someone who has left the valid marriage of his life, the sacrament, and entered into another marriage cannot communicate does in fact hold definitively.

Everything revolves again and again on this point: What must the Church salvage from her tradition and what must she, if the need arises, discard. How is this question decided? Is there a list with two columns? On the right: always valid; on the left: capable of renewal?

No, it's obviously not that simple. But there are various degrees of importance in the tradition. It was once customary in theology to speak of degrees of certitude, and that was not so wrong. Many say that we have to go back to that. The term hierarchy of truths does seem to point in this direction, namely, that not everything has the same weight, that there are, so to speak, essentials, for example, the great conciliar decisions or what is stated in the Creed. These things are the Way and as such are vital to the Church's existence; they belong to her inner identity. And then there are ramifications that are connected with these essentials and that certainly belong to the whole tree but that are not all of the same importance. The identity of the Church has clear distinguishing marks, so that it is not rigid, but the identity of something living, which remains true to itself in the midst of development.

Women's Ordination

On another issue, women's ordination, an absolute "no" has been "promulgated by the Magisterium in an infallible way". This was reconfirmed by the Pope in the fall of 1995. "We do not have the right to change this", reads the statement. So here, too, it is the historical argument that counts. But if one takes that seriously, there ought never to have been a Saint Paul, for everything new also does away with holy and venerable things. Paul did new things. The question is: When can you put an end to a particular [disciplinary] regulation? How can new things come into being? And: Can't the foreshortening of history also be an idolatry that is incompatible with the freedom of a Christian?

Here, I think, it is necessary to state a few things more precisely. The first point is that Saint Paul did new things in the name of Christ but not in his own name. And he emphasized very explicitly that anyone who acknowledges Old Testament revelation as valid but then, on the other hand, alters a few things without authorization is acting unjustly. There could be new things because God had done new things in Christ. And as a servant of this newness, he knew that he hadn't invented it but that it came out of the newness of Jesus Christ himself. Which then in turn has its conditions; and in that matter he was very strict. If you think, for example, of the account of the Last Supper, he says expressly: "I received myself what I have handed on to you", thus clearly declaring that he is bound to what the Lord did on the last night and what has come down to him by way of tradition. Or think of the message of Easter, where he says once more: This I received, and I also encountered him myself. And so we teach, and so we all teach; and whoever doesn't do that estranges himself from Christ. Paul distinguished very clearly between the new things that come from Christ and the bond to Christ, which alone authorizes him to do these new things. That is the first point.

The second is that in all areas that aren't really defined by the Lord and the apostolic tradition there are in fact constant changes—even today. The question is just this: Does it come from the Lord or not? And how does one recognize this? The answer, confirmed by the Pope, that we, the Congregation for the Doctrine of the Faith, gave to the issue of women's ordination does not say that the Pope has now performed an infallible act of teaching. The Pope rather established that the Church, the bishops of all places and times, have always taught and acted in this way. The Second Vatican Council says: What bishops teach and do in unison over a very long time is infallible; it is the expression of a bond that they themselves did not create. The *responsum* appeals to this passage of the Council (*Lumen Gentium*, 25). It is not, as I said, an infallible act of the Pope, but the binding authority rests upon the continuity of the tradition. And, as a matter of fact, this continuity with the origin is already something significant. For it was never something self-evident. The ancient religions, without exception, had priestesses, and it was so in the Gnostic movements as well. An Italian scholar recently discovered that in southern Italy, around the fifth or sixth century, various groups instituted priestesses and that the bishops and the pope immediately took steps against this. Tradition didn't emerge from the surrounding world but from within Christianity.

But I would now add a further piece of information that I find very interesting. I am referring to the diagnosis that one of the most important Catholic feminists, Elisabeth Schüssler-Fiorenza, has given in this matter. She is a German, an important exegete, who studied exegesis in Münster, where she married an Italian-American from Fiorenza, and who now teaches in America. At first she took a vehement part in the struggle for women's ordination, but now she says that that was a wrong goal. The experience with female priests in the Anglican Church has, she says, led to the realization that "ordination is not a solution; it isn't what we wanted." She also explains why. She says, "ordination is subordination, and that's exactly what we don't want." And on this point her diagnosis is completely correct.

To enter into an *ordo* always also means to enter into a relationship of subordination. But in our liberation movement, says Schüssler-Fiorenza, we don't want to enter into an *ordo*, into a *subordo*, a "subordination", but to overcome the very phenomenon itself. Our struggle, she says, therefore mustn't aim at women's ordination; that is precisely the wrong thing to do. Rather, it must aim at the cessation of ordination altogether and at making the Church a society of equals in which there is only a "shifting leadership". Given the motivations behind the struggle for women's ordination, which does in fact aim at powersharing and liberation from subordination, she has seen that correctly. But then one must really say there is a whole question behind this: What is the priesthood actually? Does the sacrament exist, or should there be only a shifting leadership in which no one is allowed permanent access to "power"? I think that in this sense perhaps the discussion will also change in the near future.

All these questions that we have just touched upon have for years been constantly reorchestrated, sometimes with more, sometimes with less, response from the people. How do you judge undertakings like the "Petition of the People of the Church" in Germany?

I already said a few things about that when we were talking about the situation of the Church in Italy and in other countries. I find that Metz's remarks in many respects are right on the mark. If I recall correctly, he points out that this movement merely tries to cure the symptoms, whereas it excludes the question that is really at the core of the crisis in the Church, which he terms—and the expression is perhaps not entirely felicitous—a "God-crisis". As far as the content is concerned, he has indicated exactly the decisive point. And when we spoke earlier of the modern consensus that is opposed to faith, I described it in these terms: God no longer counts, even if he should exist. If we live in this way, then the Church becomes a club, which now has to search for substitute goals and meanings. And then all the things that can't be explained without God are vexatious. In other words, the precise point that is centrally at issue is bracketed out. Metz then—I'm still following my memory—points out that the "Petition of the People of the Church" is on the whole met in the Protestant Churches. It is quite obvious that this does not protect them from the crisis. So the question is raised— he says something more or less like this—why we want to make ourselves a clone of Protestant Christianity. I can only agree with all that.

It seems that something like a Western-liberal civilizational Chris-tianity has formed, a sort of secularized faith that regards many things as one and the same. This culture, which often no longer really has much to do with the essence of Christianity—or of Catholi-cism—clearly seems to be becoming more attractive. One has the im-pression that the official Church has hardly anything, at least theologically, to say against this philosophy, which is represented espe-cially by Eugen Drewermann.

The Drewermann craze [*Welle*] is already beginning to abate. What he proposes is indeed just a variant of that general cul-ture of secularized faith of which you spoke. I would say that people don't want to do without religion, but they want it only to give, not to make its own demands on man. People want to take the mysterious element in religion but spare themselves the effort of faith. The diverse forms of this new religion, of its religiosity and its philosophy, all largely con-verge today under the heading "New Age". A sort of mystical union with the divine ground of the world is the goal to which various techniques are supposed to lead. So there is the idea that it is possible to experience religion in its highest form and at the same time to remain completely within the scientific picture of the world. In contrast to this, the Chris-tian faith seems complicated. It is doubtless in a difficult situ-ation. But, thank God, great Christian thinkers and exemplary figures of Christian life have not been lacking even in this very century. They show the relevance of Christian faith and make evident that this faith helps one attain the fulfillment of humanity. For this reason there are most definitely new move-ments toward a decisive Christian life precisely in the younger generation, even if this can't become a mass movement.

The "canon of criticism" just treated is apparently not so easy to be rid of. If that is so, how must one deal with it? Is it possible to wait out all these questions? Will we ever be rid of them?

In any case, they will lose their urgency as soon as the Church is no longer looked upon as a final end, an end in itself, and as a place for gaining power. As soon as celibacy is once again lived convincingly out of a strong faith. As soon as we see eternal life as the goal of Christianity instead of ensconcing ourselves in a group in which one can exercise power, I am convinced that a spiritual turning point will come sometime and that then these questions will lose their urgency as suddenly as they arose. After all, in the end, they are not man's real questions, either.

PART 3

On the Threshold of a New Era

Two Thousand Years of Salvation History—

and Still No Redemption?

The doctrine of salvation has been preached for two thousand years now, and for two thousand years there has been a Church that, following Jesus' footsteps, champions a new humanity, peace, justice, and love of neighbor. But at the end of the second millennium after Christ, the results seem to be more paltry than ever before. The American writer Louis Begley goes so far as to call the twentieth century "a satanic requiem". He calls it an inferno of death and murder, of massacres and violent crimes, in short, a compendium of horror.

In the twentieth century more people have been murdered than ever before. This is the period of the Holocaust and the development of the atom bomb. People had thought that an epoch of peace would dawn after the Second World War. One would have thought that the Holocaust had taught us where racism finally leads. But after 1945 there followed a span of time in which more wars were waged than in any previous historical period. And in the nineties we are witnessing war and religious war in Europe, and around the world we are seeing an increase in hunger, banishment, racism, crime—the predominance of evil. Of course, at the end of the millennium there are also great positive changes to be registered: the end of violent state rule in the former Communist states and the fall of the iron curtain in Central Europe, readiness for dialogue in the regions of war, a rapprochement in the Near East.

For many who reflect on the working of God and the working of man in the world, considerable doubts arise. Has the world really been redeemed? Can we really call the years after Christ years of salvation?

That is quite a bundle of observations and questions. The basic question is, as a matter of fact: Has Christianity really brought salvation, has it brought redemption, or hasn't it actually remained fruitless? Hasn't Christianity perhaps by now lost its power?

I think that we must say first that salvation, the salvation coming from God, is not quantitative, hence, not the sum of an addition. In technical discoveries there is a growth that may proceed by fits and starts but is nonetheless somehow continuous. The purely quantitative is measurable, and one can ascertain whether there is now more or less. A quantifiable progress in man's goodness, however, is impossible, because every man is new and because in a certain respect history begins anew with every man.

It is very important to learn this distinction. The goodness of man, to put it like that, is not quantifiable. We therefore cannot assume that a Christianity that in the year zero begins as a mustard seed ought to be a huge tree at the end and that everyone ought to be able to see how much better things have gotten century by century. There can be collapses and repeated ruptures, because redemption is always entrusted to the freedom of man, and God will never annul this freedom.

The Enlightenment developed the idea that the process of civilization was almost compelled to push human development continuously in the direction of truth, beauty, and goodness. Consequently, barbaric acts would no longer be conceivable in the future.

Redemption is always related to freedom. This is what you

might call its risk structure. Redemption is thus never imposed from the outside or cemented by firm structures but is held in the fragile vessel of human freedom. If we believe that human nature has attained a higher level, we have to reckon with the fact that it can all collapse. This, I would say, is nothing less than the conflict that Jesus settles in his temptations: Must redemption be something that stands permanently as a structure in the world and that can then be calculated quantitatively: Everyone has gotten bread, from now on there is no more hunger? Or is redemption something quite different? Because it is bound to freedom, because it is not something that is already imposed in structures but again and again appeals to freedom, which in turn makes it to a certain degree vulnerable.

We must also see that time and again Christianity has released the greatest forces of love. When one compares what actually has come into history through Christianity, it is rather considerable. Goethe said: It brought reverence for what is below us. As a matter of fact, it was Christianity that first gave rise to an organized care for the sick and weak and a whole organization of love. Christianity was also responsible for the growth of respect for all men in all stations of life. It is quite interesting that when the Emperor Constantine recognized Christianity, he felt it was his very first duty to introduce legal changes that freed Sunday for all, and he took care that slaves obtained certain rights.

Or when I think, for example, of Athanasius, the great Alexandrian bishop of the fourth century, who recounts from his own experience how the tribes confronted each other knife in hand, as it were, until with the Christians there came a certain longing for peace. But those are things that are not automatically given with the structure of a political kingdom. They can also, as we are seeing today, collapse again.

Where man leaves faith behind, the horrors of pagandom return with reinforced potentialities. I think that we have really been able to see that God has entered into history in a much more fragile way, so to speak, than we would like. But also that this is his answer to freedom. And if we want God to respect freedom and approve of it when he does, then we must also learn to respect and love the fragility of his action.

Christianity was never so widespread around the world as it is today. But the salvation of the world doesn't automatically go along with its expansion.

In point of fact, the quantitative expansion of Christianity, which, after all, is measured by the *number* of professing Christians, doesn't automatically imply the improvement of the world, because not all who call themselves Christians really are Christians. Christianity works only indirectly, through men, through their freedom, on the shaping of the world. It is not itself already the establishment of a new political and social system, which would banish calamity.

What significance does the existence of evil have in the context of redemption or non-redemption?

Evil has power via man's freedom, whereby it creates structures for itself. For there are quite obviously structures of evil. They eventually exert pressure on man; they can even block his freedom and thereby erect a wall against God's penetration into the world. God didn't conquer evil in Christ in the sense that evil could no longer tempt man's freedom; rather, he offered to take us by the hand and to lead us. But he doesn't compel us.

Does this mean that God has too little power over this world?

In any case he didn't want to exercise power in the way that we imagine it. This is, of course, exactly the question that I, too, as you expressed it at the beginning, would ask the "world-spirit": Why does he remain so powerless? Why does he reign only in this curiously weak way, as a crucified man, as one who himself failed? But apparently that is the way he wants to rule; that is the divine form of power. And the non-divine form of power obviously consists in imposing oneself and getting one's way and coercing.

Once again back to the initial question: The state of this world, expressed in the words "satanic requiem" of the twentieth century—mustn't it shake us?

What we know as Christians is that the world, in spite of everything, is in God's hands. Even when man casts off what binds him to God and hastens toward destruction, *He* will create a new beginning in the midst of the foundering world. We, however, believing in him, act as best we can so that man won't break away from him and so that the world can once more live as his creation and man as his creature.

However, the pessimistic diagnosis is also possible. That the absence of God—Metz has spoken in a somewhat odd expression of the "God-crisis"—becomes so powerful that man will get into a moral tailspin and that the destruction of the world, apocalypse, ruin lie before us. We must also reckon with that possibility. The apocalyptic diagnosis cannot be ruled out, but even then it remains the case that God protects those who seek him: love is, in the end, more powerful than hate.

"At the end of the second millennium," remarked John Paul II, "the Church has once more become a Church of martyrs." You, Your Eminence, have summed up the situation in similar terms: "If we do not recover a bit of our Christian identity, we will not withstand the challenge of this hour."

The Church, too, as we have already said, will assume different forms. She will be less identified with the great societies, more a minority Church; she will live in small, vital circles of really convinced believers who live their faith. But precisely in this way she will, biblically speaking, become the salt of the earth again. In this upheaval, constancy—keeping what is essential to man from being destroyed—is once again more important, and the powers of preservation that can sustain him in his humanity are even more necessary.

The Church therefore needs, on the one hand, the flexibility to accept changed attitudes and laws in society and to be able to detach herself from the inter-connections with society that have existed until now. On the other hand, she has all the greater need for fidelity in order to preserve what enables man to be man, what enables him to survive, what preserves his dignity. She has to hold fast to this and keep him open toward what is above, toward God; for only from there can the power of peace come into this world.

Today many people believe that the Church has for centuries operated in a way that is incompatible with revelation. As an example of the "sinful depths" of the two-thousand-year history of Christianity, the Pope named intolerance in the name of religion and complicity in crimes against human rights. The Church is now speaking more frequently of certain mistakes in relation to the Jews, also in relation to women. Until now, such admissions were considered a weakening of her own authority. Mustn't there be an even more unsparingly open acknowledgment of historical errors in the Church herself?

I think that truthfulness is always an essential virtue, especially so that we better realize what the Church is and isn't. In this sense, a new, sober look, if one wants to put it like that, which doesn't conceal the shadowy sides of the Church's history, is very important for the sake of honesty and truthfulness. And if, as it were, confession, assessment, recognition, acknowledgment of one's own guilt is an essential part of being Christian, because only by admitting the truths about myself can I learn to act rightly, then it also belongs to the collective personality of the Church to make such an assessment, recognition, acknowledgment. A "penitential psalm" of the Church is in fact necessary so that she may stand honestly before God and men.

I think that it is also important, though, not to overlook the fact that, despite all of these mistakes and weaknesses, the Word of God has always been proclaimed and the sacraments dispensed, and in this sense the forces of salvation were manifest, forces that also set up dams against evil. Here the force of God makes itself perceptible, a power that brings about new beginnings precisely when Christianity seems to be reduced entirely to ashes, when the embers seem to be dying out. I think, for example, of the tenth century, when the papacy had reached a low point and one might have thought that Christianity in Rome would actually become extinct. It was at this same time that monasticism blossomed anew and a whole new dynamism of faith arose. So there is a decay of Christianity in the midst of the Church, the possibility that, while still present as a form, it is hardly lived as a reality any longer. On the other hand, the dynamism of the presence of Christ is at work, bringing renewal in unexpected places.

The burden of history that weighs on the Church does seem consider-
able. On the occasion of the fifth centennial of Columbus' discovery of
America, for example, such strong emotions flared up—against the
work of the Christian missionaries—that one could have thought
these things had taken place just the day before.

Of course, in part there were also some really sweeping judgments that did not reflect the historical truth but the emotions
of the moment. I have no intention of disputing the guilt,
even the great guilt, that does exist. But new, intensive historical studies were done in connection with these events, and
these studies prove that the faith and the Church also served as
a protective power against the brutal crushing of men and cultures by the covetousness of the explorers. Paul III and subsequent popes vigorously championed the rights of the natives
and created legislation to that end. Even the Spanish crown,
especially Charles V, created laws that, though to a large extent
unenforceable, did honor to the Spanish crown, in that they
underscored the rights of the natives, who were expressly acknowledged as human beings and thus as subjects of human
rights. In this golden age of Spain, the idea of human rights
was born among Spanish theologians and canonists. It was
later taken up by others, but it was worked out first by Vitoria
in Spain.

The great missionary movements, the Franciscans, the Do-
minicans, really proved themselves advocates of human
rights. In fact, there is not just Bartolomé de las Casas but
many others whose names are no longer known. An interesting aspect of the history of the missions has just emerged.
The first Franciscans who did missionary work in Mexico,
still affected by the spiritual theology of the thirteenth century, preached a very simple Christianity that minimized the
institutional and was very direct. In addition, such a great

conversion to Christianity could not have taken place there—as we see precisely in Mexico—if people hadn't experienced this faith as a liberating power. Liberating also in relation to the cults that had existed before. Mexico could, in fact, be conquered only because oppressed peoples made alliance with the Spaniards in order to be free of domination. There are very many aspects to the whole picture, and guilt is certainly a part of that. If there hadn't been a power that gave protection and relief, so that even today there are still large Indian populations in Central and South America, then this would all have taken a very different course.

How do we explain that it took centuries to rehabilitate Galileo?

I would say that in this case the Church respected the principle of simply letting time take its course. No one needed to undertake an explicit rehabilitation. In fact, the Galileo case was raised to the status of an example of the conflict between Church and science only by the Enlightenment. It has its own historical weight, but at first it wasn't charged with such an electric and quasi-mythical tension. The Enlightenment tried to present the affair as a symptom of the Church's relationship to science. So the Galileo case was increasingly stereotyped as the symbol of the Church's anti-scientific attitude and her antiquatedness. Only slowly did the realization awaken: This is not simply past, but it still rankles in people's minds and so still needs to be settled explicitly once and for all.

The question of what course the world would have taken without the Church is impossible to answer. Meanwhile, it is hard to overlook the fact that the Christian faith has also liberated and cultivated the world, precisely through the development of human rights, art, science, and moral education. Europe is inconceivable without this fertilization. The Jewish journalist Franz Oppenheimer has written that "democracies arose in the Jewish-Christian world of the West. This historical genesis is a basic presupposition of our pluralistic world. We also have the same history to thank for the measures that have allowed the continual scrutiny, criticism, and correction of our democracies." And you yourself have pointed out that the survival of the democracies has something to do with the survival of Christian values.

I can only underscore what Oppenheimer has said. We know today that the democratic model developed out of the monastic constitutions, which provided such models with their chapters and the voting that took place in them. The idea that all have the same right could thus find a political form. Of course, before that there had already been Greek democracy, which unleashed decisive impulses, but after the fall of the gods, it had to be mediated in a new way. It is a well-known fact that the two original democracies, the American and the British, rest upon a consensus about values that comes from the Christian faith and also could and can function only when there is a fundamental agreement about values. Otherwise they would break up and disintegrate. In this sense it's also possible to make a historical assessment of Christianity that is, on balance, positive; it gave rise to a new relation of man to himself and a new humanity. The ancient Greek democracy rested upon the sacral guarantee of the gods. The Christian democracy of the modern period rests upon the sacrality of values guaranteed by faith, values that are beyond the reach of man's arbitrary will. What you said previously in evaluating the twentieth century also shows how, when Christianity is taken away, archaic powers of evil that had been banished by Christianity suddenly break loose again.

One can say in purely historical terms: There is no democracy without a religious, "sacral" foundation.

Speaking of the Church's mission for the world, the English Cardinal Newman once remarked that it is only because Christians exist, only because there is an international network of communities spread over the whole world, that the world is spared destruction. "We know that when [the Church] dies, at least the world will die with it. . . . If the Church falls sick, the world shall utter a wail for its own sake."

One may find the expression extreme, but I would say that the history of the great atheistic dictatorships of our century, National Socialism and Communism, shows that the fall of the Church, the disintegration and the absence of the faith as a formative power, actually does drag the world down into the abyss. And though pre-Christian paganism still had a certain innocence and its tie to the gods still embodied fundamental values that set limits to evil, now, when the forces opposed to evil are falling away, the collapse will, as a matter of fact, be terrible.

We can say with a certainty backed up by empirical evidence that if the ethical power represented by Christianity were suddenly torn out of humanity, mankind would lurch to and fro like a ship rammed against an iceberg, and then the survival of humanity would be in greatest jeopardy.

Catharsis—A New Millennium—

A Time of Testing

Precisely at the end of the millennium, time seems to pass by more quickly, as if there were mysterious connections at work, just like the grains of sand that, before the hourglass is turned over, appear to run at the highest speed through the neck. Many are convinced that we are living through the emergence of a new global society that will be fundamentally different from the society that has existed until now, just as the world after the industrial revolution was different from the long agrarian period that preceded it.

This is what sociologists call a watershed event, that is, the reversal of a previous direction, after which only a few significant values continue to exist in the new era. These are times in which there is really no "today" but only a "no longer yesterday" and a "not yet tomorrow". Must we prepare ourselves for a fundamental transition?

At any rate, I see this acceleration of history. Once certain discoveries have been made, everything else follows very quickly. When I think how the world has changed in the last thirty years, then the acceleration of history and the changes occurring in it are actually palpable. The changed world is already pushing its way into our present and, to a certain degree, is already here. We see how this process continues, but we are not yet in a position to survey its direction or its results.

What is becoming plain are ever bigger collectivizations. There are, for example, the European unions, the union of the Islamic world, and the attempt to create a sort of global consciousness via the UN conferences. At the same time we observe that the self-assertion of the particular [*des Eigenen*] is growing and is becoming more stubborn. Uniformity and division exist in mutual dependence. Greater and greater outrage with one another develops paradoxically with more and more uniformity. What forms are going to result from this cannot be predicted at present. I think that precisely in such a situation of rapid global change into the unforeseeable, stability in what is essentially human is all the more important.

The prospects for the survival of this planet are getting increasingly worse. Since the mid-eighties the number and extent of catastrophes have been increasing continuously throughout the world. It's becoming clearer that it's not nature but man himself who causes most catastrophes. Either by intervening in natural systems or by losing control over his own systems. Many are already talking in this connection about the wrath of God. And maybe what is happening here is in fact a certain purification, a catharsis. Maybe the old must first be smashed to bits to make something new possible. Do we need this dance on the volcano, this universal and reckless bout of "out with the old", this raging and fermenting at the end of the age, these change-filled years of world history, so that we can begin again? Is this perhaps the real task of the apocalypse?

That is hard to say. At any rate we should exert ourselves to make this new beginning possible, and should do so drawing on the forces of creation and redemption. Exert ourselves, as it were, to free up those very powers by which man learns to *limit* himself. For it is very evident that everything depends on man's not doing everything of which he is capable—for he is capable of destroying himself and the world—but on knowing that what "should" be done and what "may" be done are the standard against which to measure what "can" be done. It is crucial that he recognize not only physical impossibilities as impossibilities but also those that define the moral sphere. An education of the human race that can withstand the temptation of the forbidden fruit is doubtless fundamental.

The Church must exert herself to bring man to the point where he is up to the challenge of himself, as it were, where he can confront his physical ability with a corresponding moral ability, though we know that that doesn't come from mere morality but from an inner bond to the living God. Only if *He* is really a force in our existence will we have moral strength. We do not get moral strength simply from our own calculation; that is never sufficient.

Perhaps there is in fact no longer any chance of healing from the outside but only from the inside, healing by way of a consciousness that doesn't lie in the ego. You mentioned it just now. Might not the biblical warnings against a bad way of life perhaps mean this: It is our spiritual state that influences nature?

Yes, it seems clear to me that it is in fact man who threatens to rob nature of its life's breath. And that the pollution of the outward environment that we are witnessing is only the mirror and the consequence of the pollution of the inward environment, to which we pay too little heed. I think that this is also the defect of the ecological movements. They crusade with an understandable and also legitimate passion against the pollution of the environment, whereas man's self-pollution of his soul continues to be treated as one of the rights of his freedom. There is a discrepancy here. We want to eliminate the measurable pollution, but we don't consider the pollution of man's soul and his creaturely form. Instead of making it possible to breathe humanly again, we defend with a totally false conception of freedom everything that man's arbitrary desire produces.

As long as we retain this caricature of freedom, namely, of the freedom of inner spiritual self-destruction, its outward effects will continue unchanged. I think that this conversion has to take place. Not only nature has its orders, its forms of life that we have to heed if we want to live by and in it, man too is essentially a creature and has a creaturely order. He can't arbitrarily make anything he wants out of himself. In order to be able to live from within, he must acknowledge himself as a creature and realize that there must be a sort of inner purity to his creatureliness, spiritual ecology, if you will. If this core of ecology is not grasped, everything else will continue to get worse.

The eighth chapter of the Letter to the Romans says this very plainly. It says that Adam, that is, the inwardly polluted man, treats creation like a slave, tramples on it, so that creation groans under him, on his account, through him. And we hear today the groaning of creation as no one has ever heard it before. Paul adds that creation waits for the appearance of the sons of God and will breathe freely when men appear in whom God shines through—and who only then will be able to breathe again themselves.

It seems that a new future shock is still in store for us, namely, the reaction to the fact that we can't come to grips with the multiplicity and the dramatic quality of these strange changes. The question is whether even today a basic knowledge of Christianity still allows us to find the right answers to all these new developments, challenges, and unclarified things.

Of course this basic knowledge has to be applied to whole new fields, and that can't happen without effort, without common struggle, experience, suffering, and exchange of experiences. But the great fundamental perspectives of Christianity do as a matter of fact indicate the direction of the solution, a direction that then has to be made concrete in wrestling with experience. In this sense, Christianity is also always a constant task for life and thought; it is not a ready-made prescription that I need only apply. But it gives me an orientation and a basic light in which I then see, act, know, and can find answers. In knowing first that man is an image of God, in knowing the basic rules that are represented in the Ten Commandments, I have the fundamental orientations that have to be made concrete in the new problematic areas. And here the collaboration of many is necessary, a common search for ways to apply these values most correctly and with the least degree of falsification.

A "New Springtime of the Human Spirit"

for the Third Millennium

At the end of this century many of the once so promising models of society have collapsed. Such as Marxism (Marx: "Religion is the opium of the people"), psychoanalysis (Freud: "Religion is a neurosis of humanity"), and also the ethics of the sociologists and the idea that there can be a morality beyond institutions. In addition there are the theses of reformers who want to refashion completely the relation between the sexes, the contemporary ideas about education on an anti-authoritarian model. You yourself ventured the following prognosis a few years ago: "The new is already coming." What anticipation did you have of these new things? How are they going to look? Did you mean by that that postmodern culture, which you once described as a "culture of self-estrangement from the primordial memory of man", which is a "recollection of God", will outlive its usefulness?

That hope was expressed in my remark. I meant that the internal dead-ends and contradictions, as well as the internal falsity of such theories, will emerge. And that is, in fact, already happening to a large extent. We are experiencing the demythologization of many ideologies. For example, the economic explanation of the world that Marx attempted and that at first seemed so logical and so compelling and therefore could exercise such a fascination, especially because it was associated with a moral ethics, simply doesn't correspond to reality. Man is not comprehensively described in these terms. It has become plain that religion is a primordial reality in man. And the same holds in relation to all these other things. For example, anti-authority education does not work, because it belongs to man's essence to need authority. And so the hope that I meant to express and that I continue to nurture was that we would come to a self-criticism of the ideologies in light of the experiences of history. The hope that a new reflectiveness would emerge and that at the intersection of the self-criticism of the ideologies through the experiences of history a new look at Christianity would open up. This would allow a new conception of Christianity, for all the splinters of truth in these views also disclose new aspects of the inner wealth of Christianity.

We are seeing, however, that a positive awakening doesn't necessarily come out of breakdown, disintegration. We have already touched on that. In the former Communist countries, for example. As the economic and political situation continues to worsen, there is, to be sure, no regeneration of Communism, but there is also no great awakening in the sense that people are now saying: We must get back to Christian values. Rather, a new weariness is setting in in souls, a dissipation, a resignation: hopelessness increases. The mere failure of preceding ideologies doesn't necessarily lead to a rebirth of Christianity or issue in great, vital, positive movements. Disappointment settles in and can lead to further collapse, but can also lead to an openness so that people may be touched by the power of Christianity and regeneration can occur. But it doesn't happen, as I said, with the necessity of a sort of natural law.

At the moment we can observe how increasingly worn-out and superannuated the purely scientific, rational-materialistic world picture, which has left such a mark on this century, is. Will the man of the third millennium have to reinclude myth in his life? Is it possible that myths, which still recently were denounced as obscurantist, might be called on again in order to come to know the deeper reality, the larger connections? Just as in the Middle Ages, for example, when man lived in a world full of symbols. Nothing was simply what it appeared to be; everything took its meaning from the beyond. "Man lived in illusions," as the great philosopher of history Johan Huizinga claimed, "and because everything was illusion, man also understood the metaphysical darkness."

At any rate, we can observe a new quest for myths everywhere, also a return behind Christianity to the old mythologies— in the hope of recovering models of life and elementary powers. But there is also a lot of romanticism in this. You can never simply go back in history; you can never simply reproduce the past when the present is no longer sufficient for you. In this conjuring up of pre-Christian myths, no longer looking to Christianity—which seems too rational and too worn-out, to use that expression—we can recognize above all a flight from the demands of Christianity and an attempt to have as much of the powers of religion as possible and to give as little of oneself as possible, to have to commit oneself as little as possible.

I would not say that the myths don't contain much that we can go back to. They are visions in which man glimpsed truth and discovered ways to live. But if we merely select them ourselves and tailor them to our own use, they will not have their force. There is no religion, the very word says it already, without a bond. If the willingness to be bound is not there, and if, above all, submission to the truth is not there, then in the end all of this will simply remain a game. You mentioned the glass bead game earlier. The new quest runs the risk of not going essentially beyond that, and the new strength that is expected will not come. Instead, it will be a kind of reverie that is incapable of dealing with the major problems and forces that the modern world actually carries with it or of bringing them onto the right path. The yearning for religion is there, the longing to receive something of its power is there, also the awareness that we need it and that we live in a deficit situation. That is certainly something positive, but it is still linked with too much self-satisfaction. The humility to recognize the truth that makes demands on me and that I do not choose for myself is to a large extent absent.

Could you imagine that humanity might even experience a new enlightenment based on a proper understanding of freedom and reuniting the ends of the broken ring by bringing the dimension of faith back into life and thought? This might overcome the San Andreas Fault in man's consciousness, perhaps putting an end to the division in man. That might be a new, holistic vision, but one that cannot do without God.

A believer will always nurture hopes that a new return will follow upon periods of darkness and estrangement from the fullness of truth. However, it is a return forward, as I said just now. We can't transplant ourselves back into past periods. That is why you also speak of a new wholeness, of a new enlightenment, of retrieving the essential and fitting it together with the new. However, that is a hope which—in my opinion—is not in the offing for the near future. For intellectual forces have drifted too far apart. On the one hand, there is the fascination to be able to have this knowledge of the whole; on the other hand, there is pessimism about ever getting it. Fear of the bond that it could entail is also too great. I think that instead we are facing a longer period of further confusion. But the Christian will do his part to see that the totality and unity of man, which come from God, become visible above this fragmentation of knowledge, which also produces an increasing disintegration of life. The attempt to head toward something like this is necessary, but I do not harbor the expectation that it will happen quickly.

However, John Paul II, in his talk before the United Nations in New York in 1995 on the foundations of a new world order, also spoke of a new hope for the third millennium. "We shall see", said the Pope, "that the tears of this century have prepared the ground for a new springtime of the human spirit." What might be meant by this "springtime"? A new identity of man?

That is a chapter of its own. The Pope does indeed cherish a great expectation that the millennium of divisions will be followed by a millennium of unifications. He has in some sense the vision that the first Christian millennium was the millennium of Christian unity—there were schisms, as we know, but there was still the unity of East and West; the second millennium was the millennium of great divisions; and that now, precisely at the end, we could rediscover a new unity through a great common reflection. His whole ecumenical effort stands in this historical-philosophical perspective. He is convinced that the Second Vatican Council, with its Yes to ecumenism and its call to ecumenism, is part of this historical-philosophical movement.

The emergence of ecumenism at the Second Vatican Council is indeed a sign of a sort of renewed approach to a new unity. It is thus filled with the hope that the millennia have their physiognomy; that all the catastrophes of our century, all its tears, as the Pope says, will be caught up at the end and turned into a new beginning. Unity of mankind, unity of religions, unity of Christians—we ought to search for these unities again, so that a more positive epoch may really begin. We must have visions. This is a vision that inspires and that challenges us to move in this direction. The Pope's untiring activity comes precisely from his visionary power. It would also be fatal if we let ourselves be guided by purely negative calculations, if we didn't allow ourselves to be guided by visions that carry a positive, meaningful content and that then give us guidelines and courage for action. Whether the vision is actually fulfilled is something we naturally have to leave entirely in God's hands. At the moment I do not yet see it approaching.

Priorities of the Church's Development

Church, State, and Society

The nineteenth century, by separating Church and state, declared the faith to be something subjective, hence, a private affair. Many assume that the ongoing process of secularization threatens the survival of the faith and the Church. The time in which the state prescribed religion is now over—but isn't this ultimately an opportunity for the Church and faith? "It befits the nature of the Church", you once said, clarifying this relationship, "for her to be separated from the state and for her faith not to be imposed by the state, but to rest upon freely acquired conviction."

The idea of the separation of Church and state came into the world first through Christianity. Until then the political constitution and religion were always united. It was the norm in all cultures for the state to have sacrality in itself and be the supreme protection of sacrality. This held true for the prehistory of Christianity in the Old Testament. In Israel the two things are initially fused. Only when Israel's faith emerges from the people and becomes the faith of all peoples does it become detached from identification with politics and prove to be an element that stands above political divisions and differences. That is also the real point of conflict between Christianity and the Roman Empire. The state did tolerate private religions, but only on the condition that they recognize the state cult itself, the solidarity of the heaven of the gods under

f Rome, and acknowledge the state religion as the
ructure over all private religions.

nity did not accept this but deprived the state of its
re. It thus called into question the basic construction of the Roman empire, indeed, of the ancient world as
such. In this sense, this separation is ultimately a primordial
Christian legacy and also a decisive factor for freedom. Thus,
the state is not itself the sacred power but simply an order that
finds its limit in a faith that worships, not the state, but a God
who stands over against it and judges it. This is the new element. This can naturally take different forms in the constitutions of society. In this sense, the development of the
Enlightenment, with which the model of the separation of
Church and state appears, definitely has a positive side. What
is negative about it is that modernity at the same time reduces
religion to subjectivity—and then there is again an absolu-
tization of the state, such as becomes very clear in Hegel.

On the one hand, Christianity always refused, at least at the
beginning, to see itself as a state religion but distinguished itself from the state. It was willing to pray for the emperors but
not to sacrifice to them. On the other hand, it has always
publicly claimed to be, not just mere subjective feeling—
"feeling is everything", says Faust—but a truth that is spoken
publicly, establishes public criteria, and that in a certain measure also binds the state and the powerful of this world. I
think that in this sense the development of modernity brings
with it the negative aspect of subjectivization, but the positive
side of this is the opportunity for a free Church in a free state,
if one may put it like that. Here are opportunities for a more
vital, because more deeply and more freely grounded, faith,
which, however, must fight against being subjectivized and
which must continue to try to speak its message publicly.

Pier Paolo Pasolini saw the Church's opportunity in setting herself apart, in a radical opposition role. In the summer of 1977 he wrote in a letter to Pope Paul VI: "In the context of a radical, perhaps utopian, or at least eschatologically oriented, perspective, it is clear what the Church ought to do in order to avoid an ignominious end. She ought to join the opposition. In such a struggle—which, moreover, can look back to a long tradition, with the battle of the papacy against the worldly empire—the Church could combine all those forces that refuse to bow to the new domination of consumerism. The Church could become the symbol for this refusal by going back to her origins, to opposition and to revolt."

There is a lot of truth in that. The untimeliness of the Church, which, on the one hand, is her weakness—she is pushed aside—can also be her strength. Perhaps people can indeed perceive that opposition to the banal ideology that dominates the world is necessary and that the Church can be contemporary by being anti-contemporary, by setting herself against what everybody says. To the Church falls the role of prophetic contradiction, and she must also have the courage for that. Precisely the courage for the truth—even though at first it seems to do damage, to lose popularity, and to force the Church into the ghetto—is in reality her great power.

However, I would not want to describe the Church's role in general as opposition. She is always essentially involved in positive, constructive efforts. She will always attempt to collaborate positively so that things may have their right shape. She will therefore not have the right to withdraw into a general opposition but must rather see very precisely where she must offer resistance and where she must offer her help, encouragement, and support; where she must say Yes and where No in order to defend her own essence.

Ecumenism and Unity

You have already mentioned that for Pope John Paul II the unity of Christians is the great vision of the millennium that is now ending. The Roman Catholic Church has made overtures and has gotten interconfessional dialogue rolling on the theological level. In the encyclical Ut Unum Sint, *published in May 1995, the Pope expresses the following hope regarding ecumenism: "At the threshold of the new Millennium, . . . an exceptional occasion, in view of which she asks the Lord to increase the unity of all Christians until they reach full communion." For "division 'openly contradicts the will of Christ, [and] provides a stumbling block to the world.' . . ." Is this unity of Christians at all possible? For in the encyclical just cited we also read that "all forms of reductionism or facile 'agreement' must be absolutely avoided."*

The question of models of unity is a large and difficult one. First of all, we have to ask: What is possible? What may we hope for? What can we not hope for? Secondly: What is also truly good? An absolute unity of Christians within history is something I do not venture to hope for. After all, we see how fragmentation continues to occur at the very same time that efforts toward unity are taking place. Not only that, there is a constant formation of new sects, among which there are also syncretistic sects with significant pagan, non-Christian elements. Even the ruptures within the Churches are widening, both in the Churches of the Reformation, in which the division between more evangelical elements and modern movements is increasingly deep (in fact, we are seeing the two wings drift apart in German Protestantism), as well as in Orthodoxy. Here, at any rate, there is always a less strong unity because of the autocephalous Churches, but there are also movements of division; the same ferment is at work. And in the Catholic Church herself there are, in fact, very deep ruptures, so much so that one sometimes really has the feeling that two Churches are living side by side in one Church.

We have to see two things. On the one hand, the rapprochement of divided Christianity; on the other hand, that simultaneously further internal ruptures are coming into being. One should be wary of utopian hopes. What is important is that all of us constantly recall the essentials, that everyone try, so to speak, to jump over his own shadow and to grasp the real core in faith. Much is already done if no further inner ruptures occur. And if we grasp that in our separateness we can agree about many things. I do not think that we can come very quickly to great "confessional unions". It is much more important that we accept each other with great inner respect, indeed, with love, that we recognize each other as Christians, and that in the essential things we try to bear a common witness to the world, both for the right shaping of the worldly order as well as in terms of the answer to the great questions about God, about the origin and destiny of man.

Islam

Romanticizing orientalism has put together a picture of the East and of Islam that doesn't always do justice to the realities. However, it's impossible to overlook the fact that Islam's self-understanding is fundamentally different from the values of Western society. There is a completely different evaluation of the position of the individual or the significance of equality between man and woman, to take just two examples, in the East and in the West. Terrorist bombings by extremist Muslims continue to give Islam a bad name today, and even in Europe there is a growing fear of murderous fanatics. No one will deny that a better knowledge of and understanding among cultures are necessary. But on what basis?

A difficult question. I think that first we must realize that Islam is not a uniform thing. In fact, there is no single authority for all Muslims, and for this reason dialogue with Islam is always dialogue with certain groups. No one can speak for Islam as a whole; it has, as it were, no commonly regulated orthodoxy. And, to prescind from the schism between Sunnites and Shiites, it also exists in many varieties. There is a noble Islam, embodied, for example, by the King of Morocco, and there is also the extremist, terrorist Islam, which, again, one must not identify with Islam as a whole, which would do it an injustice.

An important point, however, is what you touched upon, namely, that the interplay of society, politics, and religion has a completely different structure in Islam as a whole. Today's discussion in the West about the possibility of Islamic theological faculties or about the idea of Islam as a legal entity presupposes that all religions have basically the same structure, that they all fit into a democratic system with its regulations and the possibilities provided by these regulations. In itself, however, this necessarily contradicts the essence of Islam, which simply does not have the separation of the political and the religious sphere that Christianity has had from the beginning. The Koran is a total religious law, which regulates the whole of political and social life and insists that the whole order of life be Islamic. *Sharia* shapes society from beginning to end. In this sense, it can exploit such partial freedoms as our constitution gives, but it can't be its final goal to say: Yes, now we too are a body with rights, now we are present just like the Catholics and the Protestants. In such a situation, it would not achieve a status consistent with its inner nature; it would be in alienation from itself.

Islam has a total organization of life that is completely different from ours; it embraces simply everything. There is a very marked subordination of woman to man; there is a very tightly knit criminal law, indeed, a law regulating all areas of life, that is opposed to our modern ideas about society. One has to have a clear understanding that it is not simply a denomination that can be included in the free realm of a pluralistic society. When one represents the situation in those terms, as often happens today, Islam is defined according to the Christian model and is not seen as it really is in itself. In this sense, the question of dialogue with Islam is naturally much more complicated than, for example, an internal dialogue among Christians.

Can one then also ask the opposite question: What does the worldwide consolidation of Islam mean for Christianity?

This consolidation is a multifaceted phenomenon. On the one hand, financial factors play a role here. The financial power that the Arab countries have attained and that allows them to build large mosques everywhere, to guarantee a presence of Muslim cultural institutes and more things of that sort. But that is certainly only one factor. The other is an enhanced identity, a new self-consciousness.

In the cultural situation of the nineteenth and early twentieth centuries, until the 1960s, the superiority of the Christian countries was industrially, culturally, politically, and militarily so great that Islam was really forced into the second rank, and Christianity, at any rate, the civilizations with a Christian foundation, could present themselves as the victorious power in world history. But then the great moral crisis of the Western world, which appears to be the Christian world, broke out. In the face of the deep moral contradictions of the West and of its internal helplessness—which was suddenly opposed by a new economic power of the Arab countries—

the Islamic soul reawakened. We are somebody too; we know who we are; our religion is holding its ground; you don't have one any longer.

This is actually the feeling today of the Muslim world: The Western countries are no longer capable of preaching a message of morality but have only know-how to offer the world. The Christian religion has abdicated; it really no longer exists as a religion; the Christians no longer have a morality or a faith; all that's left are a few remains of some modern ideas of enlightenment; we have the religion that stands the test.

So the Muslims now have the consciousness that in reality Islam has remained in the end as the more vigorous religion and that they have something to say to the world, indeed, are the essential religious force of the future. Before, the *sharia* and all those things had already left the scene, in a sense; now there is a new pride. Thus a new zest, a new intensity about wanting to live Islam has awakened. This is its great power: We have a moral message that has existed without interruption since the prophets, and we will tell the world how to live it, whereas the Christians certainly can't. We must naturally come to terms with this inner power of Islam, which fascinates even academic circles.

Judaism

Let's go on to what is perhaps the most important point in this lineup. For a long time it has been assumed that the conflict between Judaism and Christianity is programmed in the very heart of religion. But the Prefect of the Congregation for the Doctrine of the Faith has observed that "the star points to Jerusalem. It dies out and dawns anew in the Word of God, in the Holy Scriptures of Israel." What is meant by that? Perhaps a radically new relation to Judaism?

There is no doubt that we must live and reflect on our relation to Judaism in a completely new way, something that, as a matter of fact, is under way. This does not mean that the difference has been removed; in a certain sense we may even experience it more intensely. But it does have to be lived on the basis of reverence for one another and of an interior belonging together. We are on our way to that point. I think that the existence of the Old Testament as a part of the Christian Bible has always made for a deep inner affinity between Christianity and Judaism. But this common possession was also a cause of division, because the Jews had, as it were, the feeling that we had really stolen the Bible from them—and yet didn't live it. They were the real owners. Contrariwise, among Christians there was, on the one hand, the feeling that Jews read the Old Testament incorrectly, whereas it is first read correctly only when it is read openly, looking forward to Christ. They had, as it were, closed it in on itself and thereby robbed it of its inner direction. In this sense the Christian possession of the Old Testament provoked Christians in turn against the Jews, to the point that they said: You may have the Bible, but you don't use it correctly; you must take the next step.

The second factor was that since the second century there have repeatedly been movements in Christianity that wanted to reject the Old Testament or at least reduce its significance. Even though that never became the official teaching of the Church, there has nonetheless been a very widespread disregard for the Old Testament among Christians. Of course, when one reads only the individual legal prescriptions or the gruesome stories by themselves, one can start wondering how this could really be our Bible, and in this way Christian anti-Judaism emerged. When Christians in the modern era abandoned the allegorical interpretation with which the Fathers had "christianized" the Old Testament, it began to look like foreign territory; we have to relearn to read it correctly.

Our belonging together through the common history of Abraham, which at the same time separates and brings us together, is something we have to live anew, with respect to the fact that Jews do not read the Old Testament with a view to Christ but in function of the yet unknown figure who is coming; still, their faith points in the same direction. And we hope, conversely, that Jews can also understand that, though we see the Old Testament in another light, we together try to believe the faith of Abraham and thus can live in an inner affinity with one another.

Why then did it take so long before the Vatican was able to decide to recognize the state of Israel?

The foundation of the state of Israel after the Second World War corresponded to a decision of the United Nations and to a right of the Jewish people to a state of their own, a land of their own. But the drawing of boundaries remained disputed in international law [*völkerrechtlich*]. As we know, Arab refugees left the new state in great numbers and then had to live in an extremely problematic and very unclear situation between states, as it were. In such cases, the Vatican always waits until juridically clear circumstances evolve. In the same way, for example, it waited with respect to the former German regions of the East and set up new dioceses there only when the *Ostpolitik* of Brandt's regime had cleared up disputed questions between Poland and Germany. It is well known that the Vatican never established diplomatic relations with East Germany. In Israel there was also the problem of Jerusalem: it seemed doubtful that the holy city of three religions should be the capital of a single, religiously involved state. Here, too, it was necessary to wait for clarifications. Finally, a precise coming to terms on the juridical status of Christians and of Christian institutions in the new state seemed desirable.

In the meantime, the statement that Jesus was Jewish has become a commonplace even in the Church. But instead of saying "God became man", shouldn't one say "God became a Jew"? Must not Christian faith finally also accept the historical mission of Israel?

In the first place, it's important to realize clearly that Jesus was a Jew. Parenthetically, I must say the following. I went to school during the Nazi period and experienced firsthand the tendency of the "German Christians" to make Christ an "Aryan": As a Galilean, they said, he was no Jew. In contrast, in our religious instruction, as well as in preaching, it was said with emphasis that this is a falsification; Christ was the son of Abraham, the son of David; he was Jewish; that is part of the promises, that is part of the faith.

This is doubtless an important element; on this point we Christians and Jews really are bound to one another. For this reason, however, the other sentence also remains important and true: God became *man*. In fact, in the New Testament we have, interestingly, two genealogies of Jesus. The first, in Matthew, goes back to Abraham, and it shows that Jesus is Abraham's son, the son of David, and thus the fulfillment of the promises of Israel. The genealogy in Luke goes back to Adam and shows that Jesus is man as such. This is a very important element, namely, that Jesus is a man and that his life and death concern all men. The inheritance of Abrahamic faith makes the promised inheritance one that belongs to humanity. For this reason the simple primal statement, he became a man, is important, as it was before. Finally, a third point: We must add to this that Jesus himself, as a Jew faithful

to the law, also stepped beyond the law and wanted to reinter-
pret the whole inheritance in the direction of a new, greater
fidelity. This is precisely the point of conflict. There have also
been good discussions about this. I am thinking above all of a
very fine book by American Rabbi Jacob Neusner, who carries on a real dialogue with the Sermon on the Mount. He
brings out the contrasts quite sharply, but he also embraces
them with great love and finally emphasizes the common Yes
to the living God. Thus, we must not conceal the antitheses.
That would certainly be a false path, for a path that leads past
the truth is never a real path to peace either. The contrasts are
there. What we must learn is how to find love and peace in
these contrasts.

The Holocaust did not occur in the age of the Church but at a time
when the Church had definitively lost her power over men's hearts.
But now as before it is necessary to discuss and to enquire how the
catastrophe was possible at all on Christian soil. The hour no longer
seems distant in which in Europe there will be fewer Catholics than
there were Jews before the war—whose mass murder the Catholics
did not prevent.

As you rightly pointed out, that is a momentous and dark
chapter of history. And it is important to recall that the Holocaust was not committed by Christians and in the name of
Christ but by anti-Christians who also conceived of it as the
first phase of the annihilation of Christianity. In fact, I myself
lived through those times as a child. There was constant talk
also of judaized Christianity and of the judaizing of the Germans by Christianity, especially in the context of the Catholic Church. In Munich, on the day after the Kristallnacht,
they even stormed the Archbishop's palace. The slogan was

"After the Jews, the Jew-lover." You can read in the sources, in the *Stürmer*, and elsewhere, that Christianity, especially in its Catholic form, was regarded as a Jewish attempt to seize power—an attempt at "judaizing" the Germanic race, as it was said. In order finally to overcome Judaism, it was also necessary to break free of Christianity as it had hitherto existed, in order to reach the so-called positive Christianity of Hitler.

The fact that Hitler's annihilation of the Jews also had a consciously anti-Christian character is important and must not be passed over in silence. But it does not change the fact that baptized people were responsible for it. Even though the SS was a criminal organization of atheists and even though there were hardly any believing Christians among them, the fact remains that they were baptized. Christian anti-Semitism had prepared the soil to a certain degree. That is undeniable. There was Christian anti-Semitism in France, in Austria, in Prussia, in all European countries, and thus the ground was fertile. This is, in fact, an occasion for a constant examination of conscience.

Are the Jews still today the core question for the future of the world, as it is said in the Bible?

I don't know exactly which Bible passage you are alluding to. In any case, as the first bearers of the promise—and thus as the people in whom the great foundational phase of biblical history took place—they are doubtless at the center of world history. One might think that such a small people couldn't really be so important. But I believe there is something special about this people and that the great decisions of world history are almost always connected to them somehow.

A New Council?

Outside the Vatican it seems that a major council has already been long under way. Christ's message is being rejected, and it seems that doctrines of the faith are everywhere being redefined. Does the Church need a Third Vatican Council for clarification and direction?

I would say, not in the near future. I can tell you a story on this subject. Cardinal Cordeiro of Pakistan once told me how, during a synodal consultation at which Cardinal Döpfner was present, someone said that there's no doubt going to have to be a Third Vatican Council. At that, Döpfner, with an expression of horror, held up his hands and said, "Not in my lifetime!" In other words, one experience of a council was quite enough for him. He had obviously come to the conviction that such experiences can occur only at long periodic intervals.

In fact, a council, as we are seeing, is an event that stirs up the whole Church, an event that requires long periods of time to assimilate. We have not yet assimilated Vatican II by a long shot. A Third Vatican wouldn't be the medicine to help digest it.

What actually does exist on a continuous basis are the synods of bishops. I think that this is a much more appropriate instrument and a more realistic standard. A synod gathers about two hundred bishops from around the world, with a corresponding ratio of representation, and these bishops can and should try to assess together the present situation. An ecumenical council in itself, just in terms of its proportions, would be an event almost impossible to manage. One would have to reckon with three or four thousand bishops. These are orders of magnitude in which a real exchange, a real dialogue can really no longer take place. What you might call healing decisions require internal preparation. A council is not a *deus ex machina* where suddenly the right decisions are made and then everything continues on its regular course. It can only take up what is already living and fashion it into decisions. In this sense the patience of development, letting the right time and the right issues take shape organically, is first needed before things can be poured into the juridical mold of decisions and texts.

So I do not believe we can see any miraculous cure in a council. On the contrary, a council normally creates crises, which then naturally are meant to be salutary crises. At the moment we are busy with the implementation of the Second Vatican Council.

Future of the Church—Church of the Future

Your Eminence, can we expect further new statements of direction and developments from this pontificate in this century? Say, in relation to an internal reform, to cite an example. If so, what steps come to mind in this connection?

I believe that we can still expect a series of messages from the Pope. I think that the question of Christian unity will continue to occupy his attention, that the dialogue among the religions will be a major theme. Then of course there is the whole area of problems concerning social and political ethics. Above all the core area of the gospel itself, which must be constantly preached and which is easily obscured when we have in mind only what concerns the public as a whole.

The next things planned are a Pan-American and an Asian synod. I think that these will be two important priorities. If the Pope, despite the difference between the two Americas, has wanted a Pan-American synod, he intends for these continents to complement each other, to correct each other, and to find a common evangelizing energy in the midst of their differences. Issues to be debated at the synod will include the problem of the Latin American cultures, the problem of poverty, the problem of the ancient cultures and of distinctive cultural identity, as well as how Latin American cultures can achieve a Catholic unity with the Anglo-Saxon, North American culture and how both can take a common path together. I think we await an important event here.

In the Asian synod the question is how Christianity can enter into the context of the Asian religions, how the great forces of the Asian religions can connect with those of Christianity in the efforts at the close of the millennium. It seems to me that at the end of the second half of this pontificate a great amount of energy will be devoted to these two synods.

In addition, we have the program of preparation for the year 2000, with the three years that the Pope has proclaimed: a christological year, in which the mystery of Christ is to come to the fore; a theological year, devoted simply to belief in God in general; and a year of the Holy Spirit. All of this is associated with a deepened reflection on baptism and on the Eucharist. This issues then in the year 2000 in the encounters with all the Christian communities as well as in the encounter with Jews and with Islam, that is, the monotheistic religions. I think that this program—the two continental synods, and in addition the three years of the preparation for the year 2000, which is a common program at whose center is God, the triune God, and then the encounter of those who believe in God—I think that this program sets priorities that will have an impact on the world.

In 1970, in an essay on "Faith and the Future", you spoke of a Church that would also have new forms of office. That the Church would, for example, ordain as priests Christians in professions who have proven themselves.

I had foreseen then, if one may put it that way, that the Church would become small, that one day she would become a Church comprising a minority of society and that she could then no longer continue with the large institutions and organizations that she has but would have to organize herself on a more modest scale. In that connection I had thought that when that happened, then, next to those priests who are ordained as young men, proven men from the professions could also advance, that, in any case, diverse forms of office would take shape. I think that this was correct insofar as the Church has to adjust herself gradually to a minority position, to another position in society. Also correct was the prediction that in particular unsalaried ministries will probably be on the rise. To what extent, then, there will be *viri probati* ("proven men" who come from another profession) is another question. I mean, the whole ancient Church lived on the *vir probatus*. Since there were not yet seminaries, she generally called men to the priesthood who had had another profession. However, from about the second or third century on they subsequently renounced marriage. Let's leave open what forms will develop in this area. But the irreplaceability of the priesthood and of the deep inner connection between celibacy and priesthood are constants.

Will a generational change in the Church bring with it a new culture? Will there be new forms of life in the Church?

I count on that. Every great cultural shift has also brought forth new forms of life in the Church and new forms of a culture of faith. Think of the Romanesque period, of the Gothic, of the Renaissance, of the Baroque and Rococo, of the ecclesial culture of the nineteenth century, of the new forms of ecclesial life that emerged in the youth movement. What happened after the Second Vatican Council could itself almost be called a cultural revolution, if you think of the false zeal with which Church buildings were cleaned out and the

clergy and religious assumed a new look. Such precipitous-
ness is already being lamented by many today. But in a living
Church we can be quite certain that new forms of expression
will develop. This movement is in full swing. Chaff and
wheat must, as always, be separated in a process that involves a
struggle, in accordance with the words of the Apostle: "Do
not extinguish the spirit. . . . Test everything, retain what is
good" (1 Th 5:19, 21).

Do you think that the papacy will remain as it is?

In its core it will remain. In other words, a man is needed to be
the successor of Peter and to bear a personal final authority
that is supported collegially. Part of Christianity is a personalistic principle; it doesn't get vaporized into anonymities but
presents itself in the person of the priest, of the bishop, and
the unity of the universal Church once again has a personal
expression. This will remain, the magisterial responsibility for
the unity of the Church, her faith, and her morals that was
defined by Vatican I and II. Forms of exercise can change, they
will certainly change, when hitherto separated communities
enter into unity with the Pope. By the way, the present Pope's
exercise of the pontificate—with the trips around the world
—is completely different from that of Pius XII. What concrete variations emerge I neither can nor want to imagine. We
can't foresee now exactly how that will look.

*Can there also be new theological discoveries that change the Church
and can make the Church more understandable or, conversely, that
might make faith harder?*

All of that is possible. In this century we have witnessed theological discoveries by men like de Lubac, Congar, Daniélou,

Rahner, Balthasar, and so forth. Here entirely new perspectives opened up in theology, and Vatican II would not have been possible without them. Since the faith goes into such deep dimensions, it also contains ever-new perspectives. And the fact that, on the other hand, also entirely new problems can befall us is also something that we have experienced in this century; with the progress of the historical-critical method, the invasion of the human sciences into theology, and so on. We must always reckon with such events. The faith can become harder but also easier, more immediately accessible.

One of the new problems might be that even theologians are asking with more and more urgency how we can justify the idea that God became incarnate only in the person of Jesus and not also, for example, in the deities of Asia. How it is possible that a single person in the historical process can be the absolute truth?

First of all, one must say that in the history of religions there are no real parallels to Christian faith in the divinity of the man Jesus of Nazareth. The figure that comes closest to him, the Hindu deity Krishna, who is venerated as Vishnu's *avatara* (descent of god), has had many different variations throughout Indian religious history, but it is conceived in a completely different way from Christian belief in the definitive union of the one God with a definite historical man, through whom he draws the whole of humanity to himself. The Christian faith is embedded in the Jewish faith in the one Creator-God of the world, who makes history with men, binds himself to this history, and acts irrevocably in it for all. So the choice is not between Christ and Krishna or any other figure. There is only the choice between the one God, who shows himself unmistakably as the one God of all and binds himself to man down to his very bodiliness, and another religious understanding in which the godhead appears in various images and forms, none of which is definitive. Through them man relates to something that is always unnameable. In each case you have a different understanding of truth, God, the world, and man. The Christian can certainly recognize tentative attempts in the religious images of the world religions that move in the direction of Christianity. He can also find a secret working of God behind them; through the other religions God touches man and brings him onto the path. But it is always the same God, the God of Jesus Christ.

Some of the new questions and perils for the Church are already apparent. We have already spoken of the accusation of fundamentalism, which says that in reality the Church is set against democratic society, that she is an obstacle to freedom of opinion and belief, and that she works for the establishment of a theocracy. The content of biblical faith is, in any case, being more and more undermined. Death on the Cross, ascension, and the message of redemption are all called fundamentally into doubt. The disciples simply had visions, there wasn't even the Sermon on the Mount. And there is a growing following for the demand that the Church abolish herself in favor of a post-Christian religiosity.

Opposed to all these things is the force of the faith of millions of believers, who even today find in the Church's faith the way to true humanity. In the great dictatorships of our century the Christian faith was declared dead with impressive pomp and a grand air; only intractable and incorrigible people still believed in it, it was said. After the collapse of these potentates we see that these despised believers were the true witnesses of humanity and that they made the way free again for reconstruction. Christian faith has much more future than the ideologies that invite it to abolish itself.

On Rediscovering the Center—
Visions of the New Church

The Pope has often been accused of wanting to introduce a purely backward movement, of ignoring the conclusions of the last Council. But John Paul II has declared that the "best preparation for the turn of the millennium" is the "most faithful application of the teaching of the Second Vatican Council to the life of each individual and the whole Church".

He has always been decidedly a Pope of the Second Vatican Council. It was a key experience for him. He went there as a young bishop. Only during the Council did he become, if my memory serves me right, archbishop. At that time he had a very constructive role in drawing up the Constitution *Gaudium et Spes* ("Joy and Hope") on the Church in the modern world. His great conciliar experience was probably collaboration on this text, for which he was very well prepared by his philosophical work. So this document, which is probably the most dynamic and forward-looking document of the Council as a whole, became almost a sort of maxim for his life. He is most deeply convinced of the providential significance of the Council, of the fact that the Holy Spirit gave the Church new tasks here—from the liturgical movement to the ecumenical movement to religious freedom, religious dialogue, dialogue with the Jews, and encounter with the modern world. I actually find it hard to imagine anyone as affected and shaped by the Second Vatican Council as he, anyone for whom it so decidedly indicates the path for his personal life. For this reason, it has always been an absurd claim that he wants to go back before the Council. The Pope's conviction of the special significance of those three years goes far beyond what every Catholic must believe. He lived through and helped shape those years. And he naturally also notices more and more that there are diverse, countervailing interpretations of the Council. For this reason he speaks of "fidelity" to it, which is naturally a dynamic fidelity. It is not what we would like the Council to have said that must determine our course, but what the Council really said.

Is a new tone, a new sound, needed in the handing on of the faith?

Yes, I think so. The fact that there is so much weariness among Christians, at least in Europe, does show that a new tone is needed. In this connection, I read the story of an orthodox priest who said: I have tried so hard, but the people simply don't listen to me; they go to sleep, or simply don't come at all. So, something must be wrong with the delivery. That is an example of experiences that others have too. The important thing is that the preacher himself must have an inward relationship with Holy Scripture, with Christ, out of the living Word, and that as a man of this time in which he lives and which is his, and from which he cannot escape, he inwardly assimilate the faith. And then, when he can really speak the faith out of a personal depth, then the new tone will come entirely by itself.

Can we see, especially in the Third World, new impulses that, as you once put it, work against a "European provincialism"? Will the Church of the future be more African, or more Asian, or more American, in any case, less European?

That is certain. For even judging purely by the numbers, the center of gravity is increasingly shifting away from Europe to the other continents. The other continents have an increasingly strong awareness of their own cultures. There is a modest parallel to what we were saying just now about Islam. Just as Islam attained a new pride thanks to the crisis of the European-American culture, this crisis has also helped other cultural worlds to find a new cultural awareness, a new pride in their own cultural past: We have something to contribute that will be new and enriching. Among the Africans there is a strong consciousness, on the one hand, that they are still on the way, that they are still learners, but also that they have something to give with the freshness of their faith, which really is admirable, with the cheerfulness that emanates from them. They know that their own cultural inheritance contains treasures that still await their concretization. This awareness is very strongly noticeable in South America and in Asia as well. One can therefore say with certainty that the cultural diversity of the Church will become more evident and that the other continents will make essential contributions to shaping her future.

The idea that a bishop from Africa or Latin America might take his place on the papal chair is no longer strange.

No. Everyone, at least in the college of cardinals, could imagine us electing an African or someone from a non-European country. To what extent European Christians would swallow that is another question. For despite all the declarations of racial equality and all the condemnations against racial discrimination, there is still a certain European self-consciousness that comes to the surface at critical moments. But the cardinals, I think, will simply ask who is the most suited, and the question of his skin color and his origin will not play any role.

Is it also conceivable that certain dogmas or even sacraments might be pruned back, recast, or at least reformulated because of changes in the logic of the Church?

What has really become a valid statement of the faith, "dogma", cannot subsequently become false, just as, in matter of fact, even in science a correct discovery, once made, remains valid but perhaps is put in a completely different context and therefore appears with a changed significance. It's exactly the same here. What is true remains true, but new perspectives can emerge that put it in a new light. Doubtless the sacraments remain. Their number, seven, corresponds to the logic of human life, but they are lived differently in different times. As recently as a hundred years ago even very devout people went maybe three or four times a year to confession and Communion. Today daily Communion is common. The sacrament of penance has gone through very many changes in history. The sacramental theology of the Council of Trent (1545–1563), as well as its doctrine of grace (the controversy about justification with the Reformation!), has not become false, and cannot become false, but it has developed further. In this sense, constancy and mobility are altogether compatible, as the whole of history shows.

At the beginning of the third millennium, a new religious understanding is beginning to appear in outline. It is permeated with elements and aspects of the great cultures, with elements of Buddhism, atheism, cults of the primitive tribes. Can there be a new fertilization also for the Church through contemporary global currents or through other religions?

The dialogue with other religions is under way. We are, I think, all convinced that we can learn something, for example, from the mysticism of Asia and that precisely the great mystical traditions also open possibilities of encounter that are not so clearly present in positive theology. In this sense, the inheritance of a Meister Eckhart, of the whole of medieval women's mysticism, or, above all, the great mysticism of Spain has an essential significance in today's dialogue among the religions. It consists in a new assessment of the significance of what is common in mysticism (negative theology)—without, of course, leaving aside that which distinguishes Christian from Buddhist mysticism. It is already becoming apparent that wholly new elements are also flowing from the contents of myth and from religious philosophy into theological thinking—although so far the attempts at assimilation have not been very convincing. But possibilities are coming to us that open up new opportunities for theological thought and the shape of religious life.

For almost fifteen hundred years the supportive structure of a Christian environment aided the transmission of the faith and Christian education. Today in the schools, in the media, in the institutions of society, this environment no longer exists. The values of the Church and the ideas of the modern world seem to diverge more and more. How will it be possible in the future for the Church's models of life and salvation to get through to people?

You are quite correct in saying that a Christian environment is an essential factor. I would put it like this: No one can be a Christian alone; being a Christian means a communion of wayfarers. Even a hermit belongs to a wayfaring community and is sustained by it. For this reason it must be the Church's concern to create pilgrim communities. The social culture of Europe and America no longer offers these wayfaring communities. This brings us back to the previous question about how the Church will live in this increasingly dechristianized society. It will have to form new ways of pilgrim fellowship; communities will have to shape each other more intensely by supporting each other and living in the faith.

The mere social environment is no longer sufficient today; we can no longer take for granted a universal Christian atmosphere. Christians must therefore really support one another. And here there are, in fact, already other forms, "movements" of various kinds, which help to form pilgrim communities. A renewal of the catechumenate is indispensable. This makes it possible to receive training in and knowledge of Christianity. Close association with monastic communities will certainly be one way to have an experience of the Christian reality. In other words, if society in its totality is no longer a Christian environment, just as it was not in the first four or five centuries, the Church herself must form cells in which mutual support and a common journey, and thus the great vital milieu of the Church in miniature, can be experienced and put into practice.

How is the countermodel of the popular Church, which, as we have said, seems no longer tenable in large parts of Europe, going to look concretely? How are these active communities going to be shaped? Can we also imagine Christian kibbutzim in Germany?

Why not? We will have to see how things turn out. I think it would be misguided, indeed, presumptuous, to design now a more or less finished model of the Church of tomorrow, which, more clearly than today, will be a Church of a minority. But I think that many people will more or less rely on her, who will somehow, and from the outside, as it were, share her inner life. Despite all the changes that we can expect, I am convinced that the parish will remain the essential cell of community life. But it will be scarcely possible to keep up the entire parish system as it now exists, a system that, by the way, is of rather recent date. We will have to learn how to come together, and that will be an enrichment. Just as almost always in history there are also groups that are held together through a specific charism, through the personality of a founder, through a specific spiritual way. Fruitful exchange between parishes and "movements" is necessary: the movement needs the connection with the parish so as not to become sectarian; the parish needs "movements" in order not to ossify. Even now new forms of consecrated life are forming in the midst of the world. Anyone who looks at what is happening can find an astonishing diversity of Christian forms of life today, in which the Church of tomorrow is already very clearly among us.

"Pure, Pure, Pure"—The Spiritual Revolution

The world of the Church today: bureaucratic, anxiety-ridden, full of human plans. Does it need to recover intuitive thinking as opposed to the overemphasis on reason? Mustn't it compensate for a lack of contemplation and the long neglect of spiritual values? Cardinal Veuillot, the former cardinal of Paris, once said: "Everything must be pure— pure, pure, pure. What we need is a real spiritual revolution." And won't the Church win new members when she is really pure, really virginal?

In a certain sense, your question is already an answer. I have said very often that I think we have too much bureaucracy. Therefore, it will be necessary in any case to simplify things. Everything should not take place by way of committees; there must even also be the personal encounter. And not everything can be dealt with rationally. However much Christianity makes a claim on reason and claims to speak to it, there are other dimensions of the perception of reality that we also need. We have just spoken of interreligious dialogue and of mysticism—and this dimension of recollection, of recollected interiority, has become especially necessary in a hectic world. There is a well-known saying of Karl Rahner: "The Christian of tomorrow will be a mystic, or he will not be at all." I would not ask for so much, because people are always the same. We always remain just as weak as ever, which means that we will not all become mystics. But Rahner is correct in that Christianity will be doomed to suffocation if we don't learn something of interiorization, in which faith sinks personally into the depth of one's own life and in that depth sustains and illuminates. Mere action and mere intellectual construction are not enough. It's very important that we recall simplicity and interiority and the extra- and supra-rational forms of perceiving reality.

Wouldn't this recalling of the spiritual also mean having to recall the simple faith that corresponds to the basic elements of Christianity?

Sometimes it seems so complicated to believe that only scholars can keep everything straight. Exegesis has given us very many positive things, but it has also given rise to the impression that an ordinary person can't read the Bible because it is all so complicated. We must relearn that it says something to everyone and that it is given precisely to the simple. On this point I agree with a movement that arose within liberation theology. This movement speaks of *interpretación popular*. According to this view, the Bible really belongs to the people, and so they are the real interpreters. The core of this is correct; the Bible is given precisely to the simple. They don't need to know all the critical nuances; they can understand the heart of the matter. Theology with its great discoveries will not become superfluous; indeed, in the global dialogue among the cultures it will become even more necessary. But it must not obscure the ultimate simplicity of the faith, which puts us simply before God and before a God who has come close to me by becoming man.

Can you imagine that after the quantitative losses, after the apostasy of believers no longer tied to Christianity by any spiritual interest, a new quality of Christianity will soon conserve and concentrate the contents of the faith? Cardinal Lustiger says that contemporary culture doesn't signal the end of religion, and thus of Christianity, but rather suggests sketches and models that let us glimpse new beginnings of the future. "Humanity will live only if it wants to", says Lustiger, "at every moment it stands before the last judgment." But as great as the freedom to destroy life on the planet by our own power has become, the freedom to be a Christian without having to is just as great. Things are now just starting, in the Cardinal's interpretation, we are poised before "the beginnings of the Christian era". Do you share this view?

I would not go so far as to say that we are about to see the beginning of the Christian era. For what, exactly, is a Christian era? But what I can really agree with is that Christianity again and again has the chance to begin anew. I once wrote that Christianity is always the mustard seed and the tree at the same time, always simultaneously Good Friday and Easter. Good Friday is never simply behind us; it is always here, and the Church is never a fully grown tree, for in that case she would at some point dry up and cease; but she repeatedly finds herself in the situation of the mustard seed. In this sense I agree with him completely that we are actually once again before a new beginning and that this also contains the hopes of a new beginning. The task to believe completely out of freedom and in freedom and to believe while witnessing against a weary world also contains new hopes, new possibilities for expressing Christianity. Precisely an age in which

Christianity is quantitatively reduced can b...
conscious Christianity to a new vitality. In thi...
deed true that we are standing before a new kin...
era. I won't venture to make prophecies about w...
happen, whether it can happen slowly or quickly...
really do underscore is that in Christianity there ... always a
new beginning. There are such beginnings even now, and
they will continue to exist. And they will bring forth new
powerful forms of living the Christian reality.

Some years ago you expressed the hope that something like a "Pente-
cost hour" of the Church was approaching. There were, you said,
groups of young people with a relaxed commitment to the whole faith
of the Church, to "full, undivided catholicity". Do we need new
Christians who are again more courageous and proud? You once
claimed that the Church nowadays needs, not new reformers, but new
saints who are born of the inner vitality of the faith itself, which en-
ables them to discover anew the richness, the indispensability of the
faith.

To start with the catchwords reformer/saint, every saint is a
reformer in the sense that he revivifies the Church and also
purifies her. But reformer is more frequently understood as
referring to people who carry out structural measures and are
active within the domain of structures. And in this sense I
would say that, as a matter of fact, we don't have such urgent
need of them at the moment. What we really need are people
who are inwardly seized by Christianity, who experience it as
joy and hope, who have thus become lovers. And these we
call saints.

The genuine reformers of the Church who have helped
her to become simpler and at the same time to open a new
access to salvation have always been the saints. Just think of

...iedict, who, at the end of antiquity, created the form of .ife thanks to which the Church went through the great migrations. Or if you think of Francis and Dominic—in a feudalistic, ossifying Church, an evangelical movement that lived the poverty of the gospel, its simplicity, its joy, suddenly exploded and then unleashed a real mass movement. Or let's remember the sixteenth century. The Council of Trent was important, but it could be effective as a Catholic reform only because there were saints like Teresa of Avila, John of the Cross, Ignatius of Loyola, Charles Borromeo, and many others who were simply struck inwardly by the faith, who lived it with originality in their own way, created forms of it, which then made possible necessary, healing reforms. For this reason I would also say that in our time the reforms will definitely not come from forums and synods, though these have their legitimacy, sometimes even their necessity. Reforms will come from convincing personalities whom we may call saints.

New Opportunities for the World through the Church

In his apostolic letter on the turn of the millennium, the Pope stressed that "the Church . . . is able to cover the whole of humanity with her branches." The following seems important to me here: in the great need for knowledge and decision in our time, credible counselors are called for, but even more necessary are institutions, higher authorities that remain unshaken in times of convulsion. The open society we want to retain increasingly overtaxes us. It leaves us alone with its plethora of possibilities, which in turn generate pressures to decide, freedoms that are often useless or harmful and that we can no longer handle. In order to preserve the opportunities of the open society and at the same time to protect ourselves against a slide into dictatorial systems, it is probably more and more necessary to secure democracy through closed subsystems, in other words, through models whose durability and power of judgment do not rest on the opinions of the day or on casual votes.

You have raised the question of the Church's position in society's order of freedom, of her relative rank, where she is situated, what the Church can mean for it. I think that in doing so you have already stated something very important. The Church is not an organization among others or a sort of state within a state that would thus have to be formed in exactly the same way as the state according to the same democratic rules of the game. She is something different, a spiritual power, as it were. She has her social and organizational form, but in essence she is a source of energy that provides what the state can't have of itself. You know the famous saying of Böckenförde that has already become a proverb? Democratic society lives by energy that it can't produce itself. You alluded to that when you were speaking of support systems.

In my opinion, this is also an important approach to a question that we don't want to pursue any further here, namely, the question of democracy in the Church. If one thinks in this connection that the Church ought to be an imitation of the state, he has misjudged the essence of the Church. For we know that democracy itself is, let's say, a daring experiment; that decision according to the majority principle can legitimately regulate human affairs only within a definite framework. It would be absurd if it were extended to questions of truth, of the good itself. It would also be absurd if, as a result, a perhaps very large minority had constantly only to obey. In that case, a sort of oligarchy, the hegemony of a group, would once again emerge. In this sense, democracy itself calls for supplementary realities that give the mechanisms their meaning and that then in turn are constructed in such a way that they live up to their own essential task.

It is therefore very important that the Church not understand herself primarily as a self-governing body that offers certain services, but that she live, and live faithfully and dynamically, from what she has not herself made. In this way, she will give to the whole body of humanity what it can't achieve by its own decisions alone. She cannot give the world any orders, but in the world's helplessness she can hold the answers ready. The biblical images of the salt of the earth, of the light of the world, suggest something of the fact that the Church has a representative function. Salt of the earth presupposes that not the whole earth is salt. The Church has as Church a function for the whole, in the whole, and is not simply a copy of something else; she is not even a state. All of this has to be present in her life. She must be aware of her quite specific mission: to be the world's escape from itself into the light of God and to keep open this possibility so that the air we breathe can penetrate into the world.

But if the Church is going to be a power of integration that gives meaning, won't she also have to fortify her resistance against power, against the dictatorship of fashions, as well as against a capitalistic social system whose sometimes devastating outgrowths have long been impossible to overlook? Won't she also have to redouble her efforts to act as a sort of vanguard for the preservation of creation? This would provide an orientation by an institution that is not only nourished by tradition and wisdom but is also backed up by God himself.

This brings us back to the question to what extent the Church must be open to new things and guard against a sclerotic entrenchment in the past. To what extent must the Church go along, as it were, with modernity, and where does the courage to resist become necessary—prophetic opposition and all similar catchwords? But this leads to the second question: Who or what is the Church actually? For there is no doubt that all those who speak in the name of the Church, that is, the Magisterium at all levels, must practice this courage to resist.

But we must not lose sight of the correct sense of the phrase "we are the Church." The Church is not merely the officeholders, not merely the Magisterium. This phrase can be proposed effectively and credibly to the world and become a basis for action only if it doesn't remain a mere teaching, if it doesn't turn up only in Roman documents or pastoral letters, but if the word of the teacher is the common voice of the living Church. For this reason it seems very important to me that such words not be simply prescriptions from above but rather that Christians themselves learn together that in many respects they have to be a force of resistance.

The Magisterium can credibly and effectively state only what is also present and living in the Church as a whole. And the converse is also true, of course: the living communities of the Church constantly need the encouragement that assures them of their identity and through which they themselves again are then stimulated to live what they are. When we say: "The Church must be a force of resistance", then we should have in mind precisely this common obligation of Christians as a whole and not merely the Magisterium. As I said, the discernment of spirits—not everything that is modern is bad, not everything that is modern is good—is also, I believe, a very important virtue, without which the Church cannot rightly proclaim her word and perform her service.

I would like to come back once again to our present Western economic system. Do you think that this system, which acknowledges the importance only of the market, will and can survive the next ten years as it is?

As a matter of fact, I understand too little of the world's economic situation to say. But it is apparent that in the long run it can't continue as it is. First of all, there is the inner contradiction of the indebtedness of states, which live in a paradoxical situation; for, on the one hand, they issue money and, in general, guarantee the value of money but, on the other hand, are actually bankrupt, if we judge in terms of the debts. There is, of course, also the debt disparity between North and South. All of this shows that we live in a whole network of fictions and contradictions and that this process cannot continue on indefinitely.

We have just (spring 1996) witnessed this curious situation in America. Suddenly the state can no longer pay its debts and must close shop, so to speak, and furlough its civil servants, which is a crying contradiction because the state has responsibility for holding the whole together. The incident has shown in a drastic way that our system contains gross mistakes and that a considerable effort is required to find the corrective elements. But I would like to add that we will not find them if there is no common capacity for sacrifice. For these correctives cannot simply be created by governmental prescription. This is the great test of strength for societies. We must learn that we cannot have everything we would like, that we must also go a notch below the standard that we have reached. We must once again find our way beyond what we currently possess, beyond the defense of our own rights and claims. And this transformation of hearts is needed in order to make sacrifices for the future and for others. This, I think, will be the real acid test of our systems.

Your Eminence, is a historical appraisal of this pontificate already emerging? What will the end of this period signify for the Church and the world? Will more than an era end with this Pope? Will the old world some day end with John Paul II, who indeed embodies the Western world, at one time called the Old World?

Your remarks bring us back to future prospects, about which I am very cautious. The Pope himself, being from Poland, has already considerably shifted the prospects. With Poland, in fact, the frontier of the West is already pushed far into the East. The horizon is moving farther East. Especially through his trips, John Paul II has very emphatically made passing beyond Western territory a part of the Church's life. But I also think that in spite of this the Western heritage, if we want to call it that, will retain its great weight in history. For not only in art did the old Church—via the Romanesque, Gothic, Renaissance, Baroque, and so on—give mankind things of great and enduring value, but the great saints marked the dawn of forms of life and thought wherein Christianity has nobly and lastingly expressed itself, which means that man has also become more man. Mankind will not be able to do without significant components of this heritage but will only be able to integrate it into wider and new horizons.

The True History of the World

On the Fullness of Time

In the apostolic letter Tertio Millennio Adveniente *to the bishops, priests, and faithful in preparation of the jubilee year 2000, the Pope speaks of the fullness of the times. He says that the concept of time has "a fundamental importance" in Christianity. With the coming of Christ, in fact, the "last days" [Endzeit, end time], the "last hour", has already begun. The "time of the Church, which will last until the Parousia", begins now. How do you interpret this? Has the last act of the drama long been written? Have we finally exhausted ourselves?*

The passage is from a biblical chapter at the beginning of the letter. The concept "fullness of time" is taken from Saint Paul. And the idea that this is the "end time", the last phase of history, is very clearly present in the Bible. Luke's Gospel, however, extends this end phase in an extraordinarily far-sighted way when he says: "Jerusalem will be trodden down by the Gentiles, until the times of the Gentiles are fulfilled" (Lk 21:24).

The Fathers took that up; they compared history with a human life that traverses six phases. The history of humanity, they said, has now also entered into the sixth and final age. This consciousness first changed in modernity. In the Renaissance the idea emerges that now things are really starting. What has existed until now was not, say, the sixth age but a middle age; now we are back on track in real history, and now things are moving forward again. This was associated then with the discovery that the world's ages are much longer, that the world, and human history, is not, say, six thousand years old but is immeasurably old. This naturally made the "end times" idea a bit insubstantial and expanded time into the immeasurable, as it were.

The biblical and patristic view—which is based on the ancient, easily surveyable scheme of the six ages of life, each of which corresponds roughly to a millennium—has to be rethought in such a cultural context. The biblically valid basic idea that with Christ history enters into its final and definitive phase is one that we have to learn once again to understand in this context. I would say that the development of the last decades, with the acceleration of world history and with its growing threat, has brought the idea of the end of time much more sharply into the field of vision again. Not only that. We also understand again in a new way that, as a matter of fact, with the Christian movement—which from the beginning aims at world unification, in some way at the separation of Church and state, and introduces a certain autonomy by de-divinizing the world—that with Christianity a new and in some sense definitive phase of history has begun. This phase of history is marked by the awareness that the end of history is approaching, not according to calculations of millennia, but that history is on the way, and that Christ is, as it were, the end that has begun, and that the world, while moving away from him, is nonetheless moving toward him again.

This is what the Pope is talking about. That Christ brings the decisive milestone into world history itself and that, in the uncertainties of history, which are becoming ever more dramatic, he remains not only the point of departure but also the destination. Oriented toward him, we are on our way to an end. An end that is not simply destruction but is consummation, which brings history to an inner totality.

In the apostolic letter just mentioned, the Pope further states that, according to the faith of the Church, the year 2000 is not about some arbitrary date that is interesting only because it marks the turn of the century and of the millennium but is a very special "year of grace of the Lord". What does that mean? Will there be special apparitions? Will special graces be shown us? The jubilee year is also meant to serve the reestablishment of social justice; it is to be a year of the remission of sins and of the punishment for all sins, a year of reconciliation among foes, a year of manifold conversions and of sacramental and extrasacramental penance.—Or is the Church preparing for something else? The Church, it is said ambiguously, "cannot cross the threshold of the new millennium without encouraging her children to purify themselves, through repentance, of past errors and instances of infidelity, inconsistency, and slowness to act."

I think it is important to clarify what this date means and doesn't mean. First of all, we need to clear away all magical expectations. It is not as though great cosmic or even cultural or religious events will now automatically occur. We must also have the sobriety to see that the date by itself has its contingent character. Dionysius Exiguus miscalculated the birth of Christ, on which our numbering is based, by a few years; in reality, Christ was probably born about 7 B.C. In this regard, the two-thousand-year commemoration would occur at a correspondingly earlier date. This means, first of all, that we shouldn't load it with any magical stories.

But history has acknowledged this fact . . .

This dating gained acceptance, and we live with it. But it does not arise from a metaphysical necessity, not even from a strictly historical one. So this is the first point: the magical expectations have to be dismantled. The second question is: What is it then? Here the Pope rightly says that it is first of all the date of a commemoration. It refreshes our memory; it is a recollection of the birth of Jesus Christ, which was such a turning point that it could prevail as the calculation of time for the whole of humanity, in principle, at least. It is thus first the recollection of what happened, but a recollection not simply of a person of the past but a remembrance of *Him* in our own innermost selves, as a present figure who concerns us. And as the date of a recollection, and the memory of a present person—not only of a past person—and of the future, it is also an opportunity and a challenge to do justice to this recollection and to measure ourselves by it.

In addition, the Pope offers humanity, in any case, Christianity, helps for renewing itself by means of this commemoration. This is the three-year program we have discussed, which is meant to be a single effort to enter within our memory and into the knowledge and truth hidden within us. This is the one thing: the Pope offers, so to speak, a way by which remembering can actually occur and can result in presence and strength for the future.

The second thing is that he resorts to the Old Testament figure of the jubilee, which provided that every forty-nine years, that is, seven times seven years, history begins anew. All ownership is abolished, one starts afresh, and that always means universal forgiveness, return to the origin. The Pope says that if there has ever been a jubilee in this sense, the year 2000 should, as far as possible, be such a jubilee for us, a jubilee with which we try to return to the origin, which is Christ. The figures of the Old Testament also challenge us to clear away old debts, really to free ourselves from the burden also, to go back to what we were saying, of frozen economic systems, and so forth, and to attempt a new beginning.

None of this simply descends from cosmic powers but is offered as a task and as an opportunity for or from our memory. I would say that we should be sober and stay with the basic category of recollection. But we shouldn't conclude that such sobriety means that the jubilee is insignificant. Rather, we should recognize its claim and attempt to release the forces that sustain this memory, so that as far as possible it can become an effective new beginning.

But the Pope does go very far in the face of the imminent millennium. He says: "Purify yourselves, do penance", and he says, most recently during his trip to Australia, that perhaps we ought really to go into the desert in order to await the Lord's return.

I do not know this text, but I am certain that it doesn't mean that the Lord is going to return in the year 2000. For that would also contradict the fact that we don't know the day or the hour. He comes again, as it were, when memory opens itself up again, and in this sense there are ever-new returns of Christ throughout history, returns where he is present anew in history. So the question of when history has definitively reached Christ, when he definitively takes it in hand and revolutionizes it—let's leave that totally open, let's not tie that to any timetable. But what we ought and want to ask for and prepare for is that he can enter in a new way into this time, precisely through this interior openness. It is in this sense, I believe, that we must understand these things, including talk of "going into the desert". That can even be taken literally for individuals. But on the whole it means that in these times we really ought to make an effort to get out of this over-furnished, crammed world into an inner freedom and vigilance. It means, too, that we need penance, without which there can be no new beginning.

Sociologists, futurologists, and cultural critics are feverishly in search of an interpretation and a term to express the time ahead of us. We have had modernity, postmodernity, even post-postmodernity, so that it is hard to add another "post" here. Perhaps the decisive factor is the longing for what will come, and perhaps this longing will also find the new term for the time. What name should we give it? Would you have a suggestion to make?

I have no proposal for a name. I have always been against speaking of the end of modernity, of postmodernity. Those are all hasty classifications. We can see the breaks between the periods only from a certain distance. To be sure, the Renaissance formulated the term "Middle Ages" in order to say that that period was something that had intervened and that now was ending. With this periodization it interpreted itself as something new, and in some sense it was right. It is also obvious that now, with the acceleration of history, a revolution is taking place that is bringing something different from the four or five hundred years of modernity lying behind us. But perhaps we shall have to rethink the entire periodization, which, of course, is also essentially Western. For Indian or Chinese history is hard to force into this periodization, even though there are parallels. Jaspers drew attention to what he called the threshold period that cuts right across all cultures. In any case, I think that we shouldn't invent a name now for something we don't know yet. We should, on the contrary, be alert for radical changes and try to hold ready the right elements for guiding them—so that this newer time, too, which replaces the one that until now has been new, but is already beginning to grow old, will remain a time of man and of God.

To add here a final question: What, Your Eminence, is the true history of the world? And what does God really want from us? You once wrote that "history is marked by the conflict between love and the inability to love, that desolation of souls that occurs when man is capable of recognizing only the quantifiable values as valuable and real. . . . This destruction of the capacity to love gives birth to deadly boredom. It is the poisoning of man. If it carried the day, man, and with him also the world, would be destroyed."

There I was drawing on Augustine, who himself resorts to the preceding Christian, catechetical tradition, which represented history as the conflict between two states, two communities of citizens. Goethe took that up and said that history as a whole is the struggle between belief and unbelief. Augustine saw that a little differently and said that it is a struggle between two kinds of love, between the love of God unto sacrifice of self, and self-love unto the denial of God. Thus he depicted history as the drama of a struggle between two kinds of love. I have tried to give this idea further precision by saying that the countermovement is not really another love; it doesn't deserve the name of love at all, but it is the refusal of love. History as a whole is the struggle between love and the inability to love, between love and the refusal to love. This is also, in fact, something we are experiencing again today, when man's independence is pushed to the point where he says: I don't want to love at all, because then I make myself dependent, and that contradicts my freedom.

Indeed, love means being dependent on something that perhaps can be taken away from me, and it therefore introduces a huge risk of suffering into my life. Hence the express or tacit refusal: Before having constantly to bear this risk, before seeing my self-determination limited, before coming to depend on something I can't control so that I can suddenly plunge into nothingness, I would rather not have love. Whereas the decision that comes from Christ is another: Yes to love, for it alone, precisely with the risk of suffering and the risk of losing oneself, brings man to himself and makes him what he should be.

I think that that is really the true drama of history. In the many opposing fronts it can ultimately be reduced to this formula: Yes or no to love.

And what does God really want from us?

That we become loving persons, for then we are his images. For he is, as Saint John tells us, love itself, and he wants there to be creatures who are similar to him and who thus, out of the freedom of their own loving, become like him and belong in his company and thus, as it were, spread the radiance that is his.